W0016829

LUDWIG & MAE

LUDWIG & MAE

Three plays by
Louis Patrick Leroux

EMBEDDED
APOCALYPSE
RESURRECTION

Translated by
Shelley Tepperman & Ellen Warkentin

Foreword by Jane Moss

TALONBOOKS

Copyright © 2009 Louis Patrick Leroux
Translation copyright © 2009 Shelley Tepperman, *Embedded*
Translation copyright © 2009 Shelley Tepperman & Ellen Warkentin, *Apocalypse* and
Resurrection

Talonbooks
P.O. Box 2076, Vancouver, British Columbia, Canada V6B 3S3
www.talonbooks.com

Typeset in Adobe Caslon and printed and bound in Canada.

First Printing: 2009

The publisher gratefully acknowledges the financial support of the Canada Council for the
Arts; the Government of Canada through the Book Publishing Industry Development
Program; and the Province of British Columbia through the British Columbia Arts Council
and the Book Publishing Tax Credit for our publishing activities.

No part of this book, covered by the copyright hereon, may be reproduced or used in any
form or by any means—graphic, electronic or mechanical—without prior permission of the
publisher, except for excerpts in a review. Any request for photocopying of any part of this
book shall be directed in writing to Access Copyright (The Canadian Copyright Licensing
Agency), 1 Yonge Street, Suite 800, Toronto, Ontario, Canada M5E 1E5; tel.: (416) 868-
1620; fax: (416) 868-1621.

Rights to produce the plays in *Ludwig & Mae*, in whole or in part, in any medium by any
group, amateur or professional, are retained by the author and the translators. Interested
persons are requested to contact: Louis Patrick Leroux, Department of English, Concordia
University, 1455, boulevard de Maisonneuve Ouest, Montréal (Québec) H3G 1M8 Canada;
pleroux@alcor.concordia.ca; (514) 848-2424, ext. 5617.

La Litière (*Embedded*) and *Rappel* (*Apocalypse*) were first published in French in 1996 by
Éditions du Nordir under the title *Implosions*. *Ressusciter* (*Resurrection*) was first published
in French in 2003 by Auteurs dramatiques en ligne. We acknowledge the financial support
of the Government of Canada through the National Translation Program for Book
Publishing, for our translation activities.

Library and Archives Canada Cataloguing in Publication

Leroux, Louis Patrick, 1971–
    Ludwig & Mae / Patrick Leroux ; translated by Shelley Tepperman and Ellen
Warkentin ; foreword by Jane Moss.

Translation of 3 plays featuring Ludwig and Mae: La litière, Rappel and Ressusciter.
Contents: Embedded — Apocalypse — Resurrection.
ISBN 978-0-88922-623-4

    I. Tepperman, Shelley II. Warkentin, Ellen III. Title. IV. Title: Ludwig and Mae.

PS8573.E6728L83 2009   C842'.54   C2009-902840-9

Contents

For the tireless bohemians of the early Catapulte days who made all of this possible. Also, for the recalcitrant fussbudgets who inspired these plays without whom I would have written innocent pastorals.

Acknowledgements

Thanks to Craig Poile of Year One Theatre in Ottawa for having first sought out my plays and taken *Embedded* out of the French world and allowed a wider audience to discover it. Thanks to Shelley Tepperman and Ellen Warkentin for giving these plays a new life through their outstanding translation. Thanks to Karl Siegler for his unwavering support. Thanks to Stephanie Bolster for her love and patience.

Foreword

When Louis Patrick Leroux burst onto the Franco-Ontarian theatre scene in the early 1990s, his goal was to revitalize the regional theatrical institution—to create a space for non-identitary and non-realistic drama that was experimental and spectacular in form, provocative and universal in content. With the energy, passion, and intellectual arrogance of a youthful revolutionary, Leroux became the spokesperson for his generation—denouncing the political and economic establishments that denied meaningful roles to educated francophone twenty-somethings, castigating the generation of 1960s radicals who had grown complacent, deriding established Franco-Ontarian drama for having become stultifying, and calling for artistically and sexually provocative drama that dared to take risks.

In many ways, Leroux's *agent-provocateur* stance is surprising. Born in 1971 to a Québécois mother and a mostly Anglophone Franco-Ontarian father and raised in middle-class comfort in the eastern Ontario town of Alexandria, he was studying Theatre and French Literature at the University of Ottawa when he suddenly decided to devote all of his time and energy to renewing francophone Ontarian theatre. Working with a group of like-minded young artists in Ottawa, he founded Le Théâtre la Catapulte, which he directed from 1992 until 1998. He experimented with various forms—a post-modern historical drama (*Le Beau Prince d'Orange*), an urban fairy tale

(*Tom Pouce*), a trilogy on the doomed relationship of a Generation-X couple (*La Litière, Rappel, Ressusciter*), a cybernet anti-opera (*Le rêve totalitaire de dieu amibe*), several short monologues, curtain-raisers, and absurdist comedies. His early collaborators at La Catapulte are some of today's leading figures in francophone Ontarian theatre: Anne-Marie White, André Perrier, Joël Beddows, Annick Léger, and Michel Ouellette. With growing public recognition of his importance as an innovative dramatist and artistic director, Leroux soon found himself working with more established theatre artists such as Jean Marc Dalpé and Robert Marinier, as well as with Yvan Bienvenue, the Québécois originator of the *conte urbain* or urban tale. A tireless promoter of Franco-Ontarian drama and an advocate for young artists, Leroux established a provincial playwriting competition to encourage new works and co-founded La Nouvelle Scène, a permanent performance space for Ottawa's francophone theatre companies. Taking strong anti-establishment positions, he repeatedly voiced his concern for the future of Franco-Ontarian theatre in a string of manifestos and polemical essays arguing the need for re-newing theatrical forms and encouraging young playwrights.

In the decade after he left the Théâtre la Catapulte, Leroux returned to academia, completing a graduate degree in arts management (HEC-Montreal) and a masters and doctorate in theatre (Sorbonne Nouvelle, Paris III). He now teaches literature and creative writing at Concordia University in Montreal and continues to write plays and scholarly articles. While his early works were performed in Ottawa at the Studio of the National Arts Centre of Canada and the Ottawa Arts Court, more recently he has expanded his audiences with presentations of his plays in Montreal at the Théâtre la Licorne, L'Espace libre, the Théâtre d'Aujourd'hui, on Radio-Canada television and radio, and in various regional theatres. Leroux has also been a writer-in-residence at theatres in Sudbury, Toronto, and Montreal, as well as at the Banff Centre for the Arts. Pursuing his scholarly career, he has published numerous articles on contemporary Québécois and Ontarian theatre in books and journals, and serves on the editorial boards of several academic journals in the United States and Canada.

This brief biographical introduction is meant to underscore Louis Patrick Leroux's pivotal role in Franco-Ontarian cultural history. Unlike the first generation of francophone writers rooted in the working-class cities of northern Ontario and united in their quest to create distinctive literary forms in the vernacular language of their community, Leroux called for a break from naturalist drama that focused primarily on questions of collective identity and grievances. Reacting against the plays of the 1970s and 1980s, which to his mind obsessively created spectacles of alienation, dispossession, and linguistic degradation, he complained that the social mandate of Franco-Ontarian theatre restrained creative expression and artistic innovation. While he fully accepted the playwright's role as socio-political critic and community spokesperson, he wanted the freedom to explore personal issues and universal themes and to do so using normative French and experimental forms. The avant-garde techniques and intellectualism of Leroux's plays are clear evidence of his broad knowledge of European, American, and francophone Canadian theatre and literary theory. His writing—both academic and dramatic—reveals the influence of theoreticians and playwrights such as Artaud, Ionesco, Beckett, Mamet, and Albee, as well as his familiarity with Dalpé, Marinier, Bienvenue, and Tremblay (Michel and Larry). Reading or seeing a Leroux play is an insight into the contemporary culture of Ontario's young, educated, urban francophones, surprisingly post-identitary and postmodern.

The three plays published in this volume stage an intimate drama of a Generation-X couple trying desperately to live out their fantasies of love, sexual passion, and personal fulfillment. The first, *Embedded* (*La Litière*), was given a dramatic reading in 1993 and staged in 1994 by the Théâtre la Catapulte. The

English translation premiered in Ottawa in 1999. In *Embedded*, we meet Ludwig and Mae, who will both star in their own monodramas in the following two plays. After an unhappy childhood marked by a poor relationship with an irresponsible father, Ludwig studied engineering at university. Unable to find meaningful employment, he has become suicidal and refuses to leave the apartment he has shared for four years with Mae. A young actress, she plays the roles assigned to her by Ludwig's fantasies. The second play, *Apocalypse* (*Rappel*), stages the ceremonial suicide of Ludwig and premiered in 1995. The concluding play, *Resurrection* (*Ressusciter*), Mae's monologue of survival, was a staged in 1996 by the Théâtre la Catapulte and reprised in 1997 at the Théâtre du Nouvel-Ontario. Although written more than a decade ago, the trilogy has not lost its relevance and energy. The mixture of serious subject matter, cosmopolitan aesthetics, and quirky humour that characterizes Leroux's postmodern tragicomedies retains its appealing freshness. Translators Shelley Tepperman and Ellen Warkentin have done a wonderful job of capturing the fast-paced rhythms of the dialogues and monologues, with their sophisticated cultural references and frequent mood swings.

The action of *Embedded*, characterized by the author as a "cultural 'peepshow,' therefore moral and acceptable," takes place in the bed of the couple who have (metaphorically) not left it for the four-year duration of their relationship. Mae has announced her intention to leave Ludwig because he cannot or will not tell her he loves her. Despite their imminent break up, they remain in bed and order Chinese food because they are famished. When the food arrives, Mae and Ludwig continue their perverse game-playing and she seduces the Chinese food Delivery Guy, an under-employed university dropout who was a philosophy major. The seduction, performed in front of Ludwig and the audience, includes vulgar language, nudity, and graphic sexual acts rarely before seen on the Ontarian stage. The play ends with the return of Mae's cat, Victor, after a four-year absence, and the departure of Ludwig after he announces his intention to commit suicide, which he promises will be "a beautiful death. Painful, bloody, lonely." Then the Chinese food Delivery Guy does what Ludwig could not bring himself to do: he tells Mae that he loves her. She, however, rejects this declaration, preferring the affection of her cat to the amateur psychologizing and empty promises of her would-be lover. Analyzing this play, one critic wrote that its derisive and ironic tone underscores the unhappiness of a lost generation that believes that contemporary capitalist consumer society has failed them, and that, evidently, unbridled sexual license can not compensate for this failure, though it does give rise to some memorable theatrical moments, surprising for their shocking content and engaging with their witty repartee. The play masks its own seriousness with its self-conscious theatricality and literariness—Ludwig and Mae enact rather than engage the conventions of seduction and breaking up, parodying romantic discourse, flaunting their culture with allusions that range from Velázquez and Rousseau to modernist figures such as Proust, Joyce, Beckett, Escher, Leonard Cohen, and Orson Welles.

Apocalypse, the sequel to *Embedded*, also mitigates its cruel impulses with absurdist humour and witty dialogue. The action takes place in Ludwig's apartment and in his imagination as he prepares his elaborate suicide ceremony in the company of a cast of imaginary characters identified as Three Mouths, Yet Another Pope, Ludwig's Dethroned Muse (a leather-clad dominatrix knitting an overly long scarf), a Giacometti-style Cow, and an Uncannily Nubile Angel Choir. The playwright has explained the allegorical nature of this weird assemblage: the Pope represents Ludwig's Freudian superego, the Muse his id, and the Cow his ego. As for the rest of the characters, the Mouths voice his conflicting desires for happiness, oblivion, solitude, and companionship and are staged as superimposed animation over video projected onto a screen; the Nubile Angels (a nod to Hollywood's *Charlie's Angels*) are dressed as gun-toting schoolgirls, acting out the seductiveness of violence. The voices of Mae, the Chinese food Delivery Guy, and Ludwig's father are heard on the telephone answering machine. Armed only with contempt for all establishments, self-deprecating humour, and an absurdist sense of irony, Ludwig struggles vainly against his suicidal impulse. In the context of what seems to be a dark surrealist comedy, the violent and bloody dénouement comes as a shock. But this spectacular challenge to traditional values and dramatic conventions is deliberate. Leroux's intention is to open the stage up to the creative force of a liberated sexuality that will replace realist drama with a stream-of-consciousness structure he describes as "fluid, anarchic, sexual, but also rhythmic, visually dynamic, cyclical." As he says, "Au diable le théâtre de cuisine, au diable les pète-pète-tarte-à-la-crème; au diable les conventions!"— or loosely translated, "To hell with bourgeois theatre, to hell with shtick comedy, to hell with conventions!" Through Ludwig, Leroux speaks for a generation determined to "*ROMPRE, déconstruire, comprendre, déconstruire, défaire … créer [s]es propres mythes*" (to "BREAK AWAY, deconstruct, understand, deconstruct, undo, understand, deconstruct … create our own myths").

The final play in the trilogy, *Resurrection* (1996), is Mae's reaction to the news that Ludwig has carried out his threat and killed himself. The bereaved Mae holds Ludwig's father responsible for his son's self-destructive despair. Although he resented him for failing to behave "like a good father should" (and for trying to seduce his girlfriends), Ludwig shared his father's refusal to believe in love: "in their view, only desire matters: desire for affection, desire to give affection, sexual desire, desire for intimacy, solitary desires, desire, desire, nothing but fucking desire." After years of behaving badly and being incapable of showing paternal love, the father had attempted to reach out to and reconcile with Ludwig, but his first effort at responsible fathering had come tragically too late.

It is the father who discovers the body, naked and arranged for theatrical effect in the bathtub of his apartment (think Charlotte Corday and Jean-Paul Marat). As Mae comments sardonically: "One thing you can say about Ludwig: derisive and cynical as he was, he had a highly developed sense of tragedy." Recalling their last days together, she talks about the lovemaking and cruel games that were their only way of dealing with the tremendous hunger they both felt. This hunger she describes as a need for strong emotions, an urgent passion for politics, love, and the truth. They were, she says, "like all couples who always need things to be intense, who believe their relationship must avoid monotony at all costs. Even if it means living in a perpetual state of crisis." Mae's monologue reveals her passionate, romantic nature: she dreams of happiness as an actress playing strong women's roles. In order to survive Ludwig's suicide and to realize her own dreams, she must put this tragic love affair behind her. "These ancient things are no more," she declares to signal a break from her history with Ludwig, connected as it is with the collective past of an older generation (Expo 67, the first moonwalk, the 1970 October Crisis). She refuses to be Ophelia or "the long-suffering widow ... drowning in her misery"; she will write her own romantic legend, find new love, create her own happiness by reclaiming herself. In *Resurrection*, as the title suggests, Mae exorcises the past and finds cathartic release, her monologue undercutting its own melodramatic potential and emotional intensity with humour. Even as she mourns Ludwig, she mocks his self-dramatizing martyr complex, his radical political tirades, his perverse games and destructive impulses. Addressing the audience directly, she confesses her feelings of guilt for having enabled his unhealthy fantasies, abandoning him, lying to him about carrying his child and travelling abroad. In the end, she overcomes her rage, her guilt, and her regrets with her determination to write. The final section of *Resurrection* is a paean to the spirit's rebirth through writing:

Rising in me, like a dam breaking, like a volcano, wave after wave of lava rising and rising, and it erupts, up and up and up: and I see!

Finally I can see what had to emerge, my true self revealed, a tangible dream, real and fluid. If only I could open myself completely, drop my defenses. My prudishness, my fear of ridicule, my fear of myself. I see, I hear, the roar of the self surges through me.

"I will write simply, within the limits of my language. The roar does not come as the articulate cry of the poet, nor as the tirade of the orator, but rather as a flickering flame, or a porous cloud hanging in a July-blue sky."

The mask drops ... and with the trilogy of *Ludwig & Mae*, a brilliant young playwright takes his place in the spotlight of francophone Canadian theatre.

—Jane Moss, Duke University

Selected Bibliography

ARTICLES OR CHAPTERS ON LOUIS PATRICK LEROUX'S WORK

Beddows, Joël. "Mutualisme esthétique et institutionnel: la dramaturgie franco-ontarienne après 1990." *La littérature franco-ontarienne: voies nouvelles, nouvelles voies*, dir. Lucie Hotte. Ottawa: Le Nordir, 2002. 51–74.

———. "Éloge de la théâtralité, éloge de la simplicité … " *Théâtre la Catapulte, 1992–2002*. Cahier de souvenir, éd. Joël Beddows, Dominique Lafon, Patrick Leroux. Ottawa: Théâtre La Catapulte, 2002.

Hotte, Lucie."Postmodernisme et critique social dans le théâtre de Patrick Leroux." *Canadian Literature* 187 (Winter 2006): 13–26.

Léger, Annick. "Au fil des mots : Survol de 30 ans de dramaturgie en Ontario français." *Entr'Acte : Revue de réflexion sur le théâtre franco-ontarien* 1 (2003–2004): 21–35.

Moss, Jane. "Le Théâtre franco-ontarien: Dramatic Spectacles of Linguistic Otherness." *University of Toronto Quarterly* 69.2 (Spring 2000): 587–614.

———. "L'urbanité et l'urbanisation du théâtre franco-ontarien." *La Littérature franco-ontarienne: Voies nouvelles, Nouvelles Voix*, dir. Lucie Hotte. Ottawa: Le Nordir, 2002. 75–90.

———. "Les théâtres post-identitaires: états des lieux." *Canadian Literature* 187 (Winter 2006): 57–71.

———. "Le théâtre francophone en Ontario." *Littérature franco-ontarienne*, eds. Lucie Hotte et Johanne Mélançon. Sudbury: Prise de parole. Forthcoming.

O'Neill-Karch, Mariel. "L'implosion nécessaire de la violence." *Liaison* 87 (May 1996): 22.

Ouellette, Michel. "Iphigénie en trichromie suivi de Entre construction et déchéance. Réflexions sur le processus de création littéraire." Masters thesis, University of Ottawa, 2004. Chapter 1: "Œuvres antérieures, forme et thématique."

PUBLISHED AND SELECTED STAGED PLAYS BY LOUIS PATRICK LEROUX

BOOKS

Tom Pouce, version fin de siècle. Ottawa: Le Nordir, (second edition) 2006; (first edition) 1997.

Le rêve totalitaire de dieu l'amibe. Ottawa: Le Nordir, 2003.

Contes d'appartenance. Editor and contributor. Sudbury: Prise de parole, 1999.

Contes urbains. Editor and contributor. Ottawa: Le Nordir, 1999.

Implosions (Dialogue suivi de La Litière et de Rappel). Ottawa: Le Nordir, 1996.

Milford Haven in *38, volume i.* Montreal: Dramaturges Éditeurs, 1996.

Le Beau Prince d'Orange. Ottawa: Le Nordir, 1994.

PLAYS PUBLISHED IN JOURNALS, CHAPBOOKS, AND ONLINE

Le Beau Prince d'Orange (new edition). Montreal: Auteurs dramatiques en ligne, www.adelinc.qc.ca, 2008.

Moi, j'aime les moutons!. *The New Quarterly Journal* 106, "Montreal Issue," (Spring 2008): 102–110.

Everything is True!. Montreal: Delirium Press, 2006. Limited-edition artist chapbook.

Ressusciter. Montreal: Auteurs dramatiques en ligne, www.adelinc.qc.ca, 2004.

Antoinette et les Humains (ou la Vache d'Antoine). Montreal: Auteurs dramatiques en ligne, www.adelinc.qc.ca, 2004.

STAGED PLAYS
(first production or public reading followed by new productions)

Se taire (reading, 2009).

Dialogues fantasques pour causeurs éperdus (2008).

Resurrection (reading, 2008).

Moi, j'aime les moutons (2006).

Everything is True! (reading, 2005 and 2006).

Le silence de Cassandre / Le regard d'X (readings, 2005, 2006, and 2007).

Tout est vrai! (2005).

Antoinette et les Humains (ou la Vache d'Antoine) (2002 and 2006).

Embedded (1999).

Alain Lalonde, barbier (1998).

La "band" à tout casser (1998–2000).

La nuit blanche de Martin Shakespeare (reading, 1998).

L'École Guigues 97 (1997).

Ottawa-les-bains sens dessous dessus (1997 and 2007).

Les esclaves de Meïkneïff (radio drama, in collaboration, 1996).

Milford Haven (1996).

Ressusciter (1996 and 1997).

Tom Pouce, version fin de siècle (1996, 1997, and 2006).

Miss Louisiana (excerpts, 1995).

Rappel (1995 and 2010).

Le rêve totalitaire de dieu l'amibe (1995 and 1996).

L'Impuissant (in collaboration, 1994).

La Litière (1994).

Le Beau Prince d'Orange (1993 and reading, 2007).

Quatre ans, à peine (reading, 1993).

Tu décroches? (in collaboration, 1993).

Dialogue (1992, 2006, and 2008).

Les enfants du culte (six radio plays, 1992–1993).

J'ai quelque chose à te dire … (1992–1998, and 2005).

Villageoise monologuerie (reading, 1992).

EMBEDDED

(*La Litière*)

La Litière was first produced in 1994 by Théâtre la Catapulte. It opened on May 11 in the Léonard-Beaulne Studio at the University of Ottawa and was directed by Benoît Gauthier. Cast and crew were as follows:

MAE . . . . Chantal Aubut
LUDWIG . . . . Claude Lavoie
LE LIVREUR DE CHINOIS . . . . Marc Thibaudeau
Assistant Director . . . . Dominik McNicoll
Set Design . . . . Patrick Leroux
Lighting . . . . Jules Ducharme
Music . . . . Roch Archambault
Costumes and Props . . . . Sophie Tremblay
Backdrop and Poster . . . . Sylvio Boudreau

A staged reading of *Embedded* took place in June 1999 as part of the On the Verge festival of new plays at the National Arts Centre Studio. It was directed by Linda Balduzzi, with Richard Gélinas as Ludwig, Jennifer Roberts-Smith as Mae, and John Gordon as the Chinese Delivery Guy.

Embedded was first produced by Year One Theatre at the Arts Court in Ottawa, Ontario from September 30 to October 9, 1999. It was produced by Craig Poile and directed by Annick Léger. Cast and crew were as follows:

LUDWIG . . . . Richard Gélinas
MAE . . . . Nicole Blundell
CHINESE DELIVERY GUY . . . . Darryl Bennett
Set Design . . . . Shelagh Corbett
Lighting Design . . . . David Magladry
Assistant Director . . . . Tara Landry

Stage Manager . . . . Lorrie Beaton
Production Assistant . . . . Lesley Buxton
Set Builder . . . . Ross Imrie
Technician . . . . Paul Auclair

In the couple's bed.

Everything is draped in white.

Milky light.

Behind the bed, behind that milky light, behind all that whiteness, are vertical blinds. The space is surrounded by walls fitted with peepholes, perhaps, or windows: one per audience member. It's a cultural "peepshow," therefore moral and acceptable.

Cinematic intimacy in the theatre.

A sense of melancholy.

Perverse humour.

Endless games. Always these games. Intricate, multi-layered games: will we ever know who's playing, who isn't playing, who's who in this game of cat and mouse, and when the tables are turned? Always these games. Endless games. Games to compensate for the inability to love, and, even more, for the inconvenience of being alive.

The bed is littered with sheets and pillows, knick knacks, a guitar, and a good deal of melancholy.

MAE and LUDWIG are also in bed. They've been there forever, or so it seems.

The author knows they've been there for four years.

Before the bed, they were both twenty years old.

Later on, the CHINESE DELIVERY GUY will arrive. Or, rather, the CHINESE FOOD DELIVERY GUY.

Then, the cat. Independently of the DELIVERY GUY, the tom-cat.

And finally, the inevitable.

But first, the couple …

I

When Myth No Longer Suffices

In the semi-darkness.
The final moments of passionate lovemaking. The sheets are wrinkled and damp, effusions still enveloping the room.
The couple, sated, exhausted, is staring at the ceiling. Time takes the silences that are its due.

MAE
I feel good.

LUDWIG
With me?

MAE
With you. Right now.

A beat.

LUDWIG
Four years ago I'd have told you I love you.

A beat.

MAE
I'd have done the same.

LUDWIG
Four years ago?

MAE
(*non-committal*) Whatever.

A beat.

LUDWIG
    Mae?

MAE
    Ludwig?

LUDWIG
    Hold me. Lie close to me.

MAE
    Like we would have four years ago? Four years ago in
    this very bed, the bed of our first weekend, that first
    weekend of passion?

LUDWIG
    Mae, you're mythologizing again. Very nice
    mythologizing, mind you, but it's myth all the same.

        A beat.

MAE
    I'm going to leave you one day. You know that, don't you.

LUDWIG
    And the day after, I'll slit my wrists.

MAE
    Don't start, Ludwig.

LUDWIG
    I won't start, Mae. Good night.

MAE
    Good night.

        *Night falls. Time envelops, then numbs LUDWIG, but
        doesn't manage to soothe his girlfriend. MAE can't sleep.
        Her restlessness wakes LUDWIG. Their voices float in the
        night.*

LUDWIG

Are you going to toss and turn all night? I'd like to get some sleep.

MAE

I can't sleep.

LUDWIG

Just try.

MAE

You do realize it isn't working, Ludwig.

LUDWIG

What are you on about now?

MAE

Us. We're like an old married couple. Except the passion died before we ever got near the altar.

LUDWIG

Shit, not again! Yes, I know, we used to love each other. You, you used to cast endearments at me, complete with synonyms and subjective definitions. From what it seems, I've only cast you into misery. I know the story …

MAE

(*pleading*) Ludwig!

LUDWIG

(*indifferent*) Mae?

MAE

I'm leaving you.

LUDWIG

Right now? What time is it?

MAE

No. Not right this minute. I don't know what time it is.

LUDWIG

It must be at least three or four in the morning.

MAE

Did you hear me, Ludwig? I'm leaving you!

LUDWIG

Yes, you're leaving me, but not right this minute. Let me know before you slam the door, all right; I'll go get grandpa's old straight razor and we'll end things once and for all. So when's the big departure?

MAE

Tomorrow?

LUDWIG

At dawn?

MAE

As soon as I get out of bed.

LUDWIG

Before or after your shower?

MAE

After.

LUDWIG

Before or after breakfast?

MAE

After.

LUDWIG

Before or after coffee?

MAE
>Is there any left?

LUDWIG
>Freshly ground.

MAE
>After. I'll leave you after we've had coffee.

>>*A beat. Now that the crisis has been postponed, LUDWIG becomes drowsy again.*

LUDWIG
>Well then, good night.

MAE
>Right, good night.

>>*Silence.*

>>*Dawn colours the stage. LUDWIG awakens. MAE had been watching him sleep. She smiles; he doesn't. He even hides his face under the pillow.*

LUDWIG
>Damn, it's morning. I don't feel like offing myself.

MAE
>It's Saturday, we could always stay in bed.

LUDWIG
>I don't have a job, it's always Saturday for me. I can stay in bed every day.

MAE
>But not with me.

LUDWIG
>Not with you, that's true.

Silence.

LUDWIG
Did you take your shower? (*She doesn't answer.*) Have you had your coffee? (*Still, that silence.*) Now what?

MAE
Nothing. Same as before.

LUDWIG
Same as before.

A beat.

LUDWIG
I'm hungry.

MAE
There's no hurry. Don't think about it.

LUDWIG
I won't.

Silence.

MAE
It's raining outside.

LUDWIG
Raining …

MAE
Might as well stay in bed.

LUDWIG
It never rains in bed.

Silence.

MAE
That phone call you got yesterday, who was it?

LUDWIG
I don't know ... Which one?

MAE
The one that rattled you. The one that plunged you into
utter wordlessness the entire evening. The one you didn't
want to talk about.

LUDWIG
Oh yeah ... That one.

MAE
That one.

A beat.

LUDWIG
It was no one.

MAE
No one?

LUDWIG
A woman.

MAE
A woman.

LUDWIG
A friend.

MAE
Do I know her?

LUDWIG
A former ... friend.

MAE
　An ex-girlfriend?

LUDWIG
　A former woman friend.

MAE
　An ex-lover? (*A beat.*) The blonde with brown eyes?

LUDWIG
　The one I was in love with.

MAE
　In love with?

　　Silence. Gaping wounds.

MAE
　What did she want?

LUDWIG
　Nothing.

MAE
　So, she gave *you* a call.

LUDWIG
　She just wanted to chat.

MAE
　… about nothing?

LUDWIG
　She was lonely.

MAE
　And you?

LUDWIG
　I talked to her.

MAE
Were *you* lonely?

LUDWIG
For her?

MAE
For her.

LUDWIG
Yeah.

MAE
Well?

LUDWIG
(*mockingly*) Alas!

MAE
Are you lonely now?

LUDWIG
What's wrong with you? An ex-girlfriend calls, just to
say hello, and you start acting all jealous!

MAE
An ex-girlfriend—the one you were IN LOVE WITH—
the ONLY one EVER—calls, then after two or three
stutters you hang up on her, you unplug the phone and
you shut yourself in the bedroom. I come to console you.
You push me away. I try again; you deign to look at me.
Finally, you decide you feel like fucking.
(*sarcastic*) Because His Nibs doesn't make love: he *fucks*.
Note the wording—let's call a spade a spade. You've been
telling me about her for four years. You talk about her as
though she were a goddess. I think you stopped living
when the two of you broke up. What's keeping you from
breaking up with me? Maybe then you'd realize how

much you loved me too. (*Silence.*) Why are you still with me if she's the one you're in love with?

A beat.

LUDWIG
I remind you of her.

MAE
I remind you of her because of what I'm saying right now, or you're with me because I look like her?

LUDWIG lies with his head on MAE's belly. She hesitates, then strokes his hair.

MAE
I love you. Can't you understand that? I love you!

Silence.

LUDWIG
(*weakly*) What about your coffee?

MAE
(*annoyed*) The coffee can wait.

Silence. MAE is still stroking LUDWIG's hair.

MAE
You don't tell me stories anymore.

LUDWIG
I don't?

MAE
Tell me a story.

LUDWIG

Yyyeah. A story … Let me think … No. I can't think of any. No stories. Only anecdotes.

MAE

Let's hear some anecdotes then.

LUDWIG

I can only think of weird ones.

MAE

Those are the best.

LUDWIG

Morbid ones, actually.

MAE

Tell me.

LUDWIG

On Thursday Eric told me he wanted to kill himself.

MAE

Eric?!

LUDWIG

Everyone seems to feel like killing themselves these days.

MAE

Who do you mean, everyone?

Silence.

LUDWIG

Did you know that hanging is supposed to give you a hard on?

MAE

Did you read that in Godot?

LUDWIG
> In what?

MAE
> In Godot—*Waiting for Godot*—Vladimir and Estragon
> don't have anything to do, so, to pass the time, they
> decide to hang themselves. One of the pros is that it's ...

MAE & LUDWIG
> ... supposed to give you a hard-on.

> *A beat.*

LUDWIG
> Who's Godot?

MAE
> We could be here a long time.

LUDWIG
> Why?

MAE
> Godot is who Vladimir and Estragon are waiting for.

LUDWIG
> Who're they?

MAE
> Characters in a play.

LUDWIG
> Honestly, Mae, I open up about my suicidal anguish and
> you ramble on about theatre.

MAE
> You're the one who heard dying gives you a hard-on—
> I'm just providing the reference.

A beat.

LUDWIG
Yeah, I've been thinking about it.

MAE
About what?

LUDWIG
Suicide.

MAE
Do you want to talk about it?

LUDWIG
No, never mind. I don't know why I think about it. It's always there.

MAE
What exactly?

LUDWIG
Wanting to die.

Silence.

LUDWIG
Four years ago no one wanted to kill themselves.

MAE
Four years ago we were still enjoying life.

LUDWIG
Four years ago we used to tell each other the silliest things.

MAE
Four years ago we didn't think they were so silly.

LUDWIG
Four years ago we believed in love and other delusions.

MAE
Four years ago we had no right to kill ourselves.

A beat.

LUDWIG
I thought about asking you to kill me.

MAE
Why?

LUDWIG
As an act of love.

MAE
You wanted to ask me to kill you!

LUDWIG
Yes, but that was before—when we weren't going to break up, when everything was rosy, when everything was going well, when we were a couple.

MAE
We're still a couple.

LUDWIG
Well, since we've decided to break up …

Silence.

MAE
I would have done it.

LUDWIG
Really?

MAE

Before, when we weren't going to break up, when everything was rosy, when we were a couple.

LUDWIG

You would have killed me, out of love?

MAE

Yes, hypothetically.

LUDWIG

I would have loved you then, in the same way.

MAE

Hypothetically?

LUDWIG

Yes, before—four years ago, maybe, or something like that—I don't know, yeah.

MAE

Let's have sex, Ludwig. But let's take it slow.

LUDWIG

Turn off the light.

MAE

It's daylight.

LUDWIG

Lower the blind, then.

MAE

Why?

LUDWIG

Don't you want to have sex?

MAE
> Four years ago we used to turn on all the lights, we'd open the curtains wide and we'd crank up Beethoven full blast.

LUDWIG
> Four years ago we were beautiful.

MAE
> We're still beautiful! Let me love you.

LUDWIG
> Lower the blind.

MAE
> No.

LUDWIG
> Fine.

> *He turns his back to her, as though he is going to sleep.*

MAE
> You're such an asshole!

> *Silence.*

LUDWIG
> I'm hungry.

MAE
> Don't think about it.

LUDWIG
> All right, I won't think about it. (*Silence.*) Aren't you hungry?

MAE

Yes, I'm hungry, Ludwig, but you know as well as I do we can't get out of bed.

LUDWIG

(*candid*) Because then you'd have to take a shower, we'd have to have breakfast, we'd have to drink our freshly ground coffee, you'd have to leave me, and I'd have to slit my wrists and bleed to death.

MAE

Yes, in a manner of speaking ...

LUDWIG

Why don't we simply call a "time-out," just long enough for me to make a few pieces of toast with Cheez Whiz?

MAE

It's not a game, Ludwig, I'm serious.

LUDWIG

Look, I could put my hands like *this* (*he makes a "T" with his hands*) till I've eaten my snack.

MAE

How would you spread the Cheez Whiz?

LUDWIG

Very simple! I'd just have to take off a sock, place the knife between my toes, then merrily whiz up my toast!

A beat.

MAE

I'd really like us to be a normal couple.

LUDWIG

We are a normal couple.

MAE

I'm sure other couples don't complicate their lives by
intellectualizing everything, let alone figuring out ways
to spread Cheez Whiz on their toast with their feet!

LUDWIG

Come on. We spend our time whispering nonsense to
each other, lying in bed, waiting for the other to finally
sneak away—like every other couple in the world.

MAE

Except that we take *our* nonsense seriously.

LUDWIG

Like every other couple in the world.

    Silence.

MAE

I have nothing more to say.

LUDWIG

Me neither, but I could really go for some toast.

MAE

Ludwig, don't start.

LUDWIG

(*sulking*) I won't start.

    Silence.

MAE

Shall we make love?

LUDWIG

Shall we do what?

MAE
You know what I mean!

A beat.

LUDWIG
Sure, why not?

He gets up, lowers the blind. Half-darkness. We hear Beethoven.

MAE
Not so fast, gently.

The sheets rustle. A few seconds, then …

LUDWIG
Fuck!

MAE
It doesn't matter.

LUDWIG
It had to happen this morning.

LUDWIG gets up, violently yanks the window blind. He pulls up his pyjama bottoms. MAE remains naked under the sheets. LUDWIG lies down again, furious.

LUDWIG
It's our last fuck, so of course, the Good Lord blesses me with a premature ejaculation.

MAE
(*beseeching the all-powerful Father*) Father! Why hast thou forsaken him?

LUDWIG
It's not funny!

MAE
No! It's a tragedy!

She laughs softly. He doesn't find it comical.

MAE
(*feline*) We could always start over again. You've been
known to come more than once. You remember, don't
you?

LUDWIG
I don't feel like it.

MAE
Fine.

Silence.

MAE
(*gaily*) Do you want to play—

LUDWIG
I don't want to play anymore.

Silence.

MAE
You don't even want to play—

LUDWIG
I said—

MAE
(*cutting him off gaily*) How about jumping up and down
on the bed like crazy till the springs pop?

LUDWIG
I'm too weak. I'm too hungry.

MAE
    I could give you a massage, like I used to.

LUDWIG
    No.

MAE
    Fine. (*Silence.*) Shall we listen to some music?

LUDWIG
    If you want …

MAE
    No, never mind. *You* play some.

LUDWIG
    I don't feel like it.

MAE
    Not even for me?

LUDWIG
    No.

MAE
    Ludwig?

        A beat.

MAE
    What do you want?

LUDWIG
    Are we breaking up or aren't we?

MAE
    (*playing innocent*) It's the breakup that's making you so
    tense. I'd like us to stay together, Ludwig, but we have
    things to work out. (*A beat. LUDWIG doesn't answer.*) A lot

of things. (*A beat. LUDWIG still doesn't answer.*) I'd very simply like us to be able to love each other. That's all.

LUDWIG
I can't.

MAE
You sound so defeatist. What's happened to you?

LUDWIG
I'm sick and tired of pretending all the time!

MAE
I've never asked you to pretend …

LUDWIG
And yet we never get out of bed. We're still in bed, for God's sake!

MAE
That's what's upsetting you? Fine, we'll get out of bed, we'll work things out and we'll get on with our relationship.

LUDWIG
Right. We'll get out of bed, we'll each get our shit together, you'll get on with your life: you'll find yourself a nice apartment, a new guy, and everything you need … As for me, I'll do what you've been keeping me from doing for far too long.

He is about to leave.

MAE
No. Stay. We'll talk.

LUDWIG
About what?

MAE
About us.

LUDWIG
We've already said all there is to say.

He gets out of bed; she holds him back.

MAE
Don't go!

LUDWIG
How many more days in bed? How long until we're through?

MAE
We're already through.

LUDWIG
Then leave.

MAE
You leave. You can't throw me out.

LUDWIG
Fine. All we have to do is be civilized, and stop talking to each other.

MAE
No.

LUDWIG
Then all we have to do is be civilized and keep talking to each other.

MAE
No.

LUDWIG
Then all we have to do is be *un*civilized and make each other miserable till one of us has a nervous breakdown.

MAE
No.

LUDWIG
Then all we have to do is move into friends' places and let our lawyers fight it out.

MAE
No.

LUDWIG
Then we just have to stay shut up in this godforsaken room and tear each other apart.

A beat.

MAE
Why don't we take a trip together.

LUDWIG
A trip? What for?

MAE
To go away.

LUDWIG
Go away together …

MAE
That's right, go away together.

LUDWIG
What would we do, on a trip?

MAE
We could sightsee. What do you think?

LUDWIG
Sightsee.

MAE
It's a nice idea, isn't it? Go away. Spend some time together. Have fun! See new things …

LUDWIG
(*cynical*) Good idea! We could end up in bed for a weekend, talking about our relationship. And not just anywhere either! In San Francisco, Santiago, Venice, Sydney, Kuala Lumpur, gee … And then why not Iqaluit, while we're at it!?

MAE
Ludwig, I don't want us to break up.

LUDWIG
Well, I do.

Silence.

MAE
(*her eyes full of tears*) Ludwig, I'm pregnant.

LUDWIG
Again?

MAE
What do you mean, again?

LUDWIG
You've already pulled that stunt—the pregnancy scare.

MAE
This time it's true, I swear!

LUDWIG
Uh huh. (*Silence.*) When is it due?

MAE
I'm not sure. (*A beat.*) I was thinking of naming her
Mary.

LUDWIG
No.

MAE
Matthew, then.

LUDWIG
No.

MAE
What's the matter, you don't want kids? (*He doesn't
answer.*) You don't like biblical names?

LUDWIG
Why are you testing me?

MAE
You don't believe me?

LUDWIG
No, I don't.

MAE
Don't you care about me? (*A beat.*) Then I don't care
about you either. I haven't had a life for four years ... as
long as I've been with you. But now, I'll have to get a life
because I'm pregnant!

    Silence.

LUDWIG
Ever heard of the Galápagos Islands?

MAE
Yes …

LUDWIG
Apparently you can visit a kind of prehistoric wildlife reserve.

A beat.

MAE
You'd really like to go?

LUDWIG
Why not?

She hugs him. She rejoices. Caresses.

LUDWIG
So tell me, is it true about the kid?

MAE
I think so.

LUDWIG
You think so? You're not sure?

MAE
Uh …

LUDWIG
You're not sure!

MAE
Shhh, calm down.

LUDWIG
Are you pregnant, yes or no?

MAE

I think so, but I'm not sure. I'm pretty late …

Silence.

MAE

When do we leave for the Galápagos? (*A beat.*) You want to leave me, is that it? You're leaving me …

LUDWIG

Listen, last night *you* were the one leaving *me*.

MAE

Forget about last night. If you're going to leave me, just do it...

Silence.

MAE

What do you intend to do?

LUDWIG

Ultimately? Do myself in.

MAE

Yes, I know, but before that, before you slit your wrists, what are you going to do?

LUDWIG

Move.

MAE

And after that, what are you going to do with your life?

LUDWIG

I'm going to find myself.

MAE

You? You'll find yourself at the bar.

LUDWIG
It's a beginning.

MAE
Are you going to start drinking again?

LUDWIG
Absolutely.

MAE
Fuck other girls, left and right.

LUDWIG
And in between.

MAE
Do drugs?

LUDWIG
But of course.

MAE
Cruise the bars on weeknights: the wall of speakers …
LUDWIG
Vibrating …

MAE
Pounding …

LUDWIG
Smoke …

MAE
The air thick with it …

LUDWIG
Thick with sex …

MAE
　　She doesn't have a name …

LUDWIG
　　But what a body!

MAE
　　The lights whirl like meteors to remind us where we are.

LUDWIG
　　I'm checking out the action.

MAE
　　So is she.

LUDWIG
　　I want to get another glimpse of her.

MAE
　　The dance floor between them oozes beer and sweat.

LUDWIG
　　Hundreds of moist crotches writhe in their CK undies.

MAE
　　She slips into the crowd.

LUDWIG
　　I push into it too.

MAE
　　The pulsing of legs, arms, butts, on the dance floor
　　caresses her.

LUDWIG
　　I'm praying that—

MAE
　　What?

LUDWIG
Nothing, no one … I want it.

MAE
Everybody wants it.

LUDWIG
The music dies down.

MAE
Our hips are still thrusting.

LUDWIG
The illusion crumbles.

MAE
The line-up forms.

LUDWIG
Against the wall.

MAE
It's closing time …

LUDWIG
Drunk, horny, my head spinning …

MAE
You get in line …

LUDWIG
And I see her again.

MAE
Their eyes meet … for just a few seconds.

LUDWIG
Long enough.

MAE
　　She follows him.

LUDWIG
　　(*breaking out of the game*) Hey, I'm the one who followed
　　her.

MAE
　　(*corrects herself*) They let themselves be swept away by
　　their desire.

LUDWIG
　　The unbearable carnality of desire.

MAE
　　They come to "know" each other.

LUDWIG
　　I get my release.

MAE
　　She falls asleep.

　　　　A beat.

LUDWIG
　　The next morning.

MAE
　　With a smile, she wishes him good morning.

LUDWIG
　　What am I doing here?

MAE
　　She offers him some juice.

LUDWIG
　　I smell of cigarettes, beer, and sweat.

MAE
　She wants to kiss him.

LUDWIG
　She smells of cigarettes, beer, sweat, and hairspray.

MAE
　He pulls away, but seems to appreciate the juice.

LUDWIG
　I don't remember her name.

MAE
　"Next time," he teases, "I'll remember your name!"

LUDWIG
　"Next time." I blew it.

MAE
　Next time …

LUDWIG
　She hangs onto those words.

MAE
　I imagine those words coming from his heart.

LUDWIG
　She lays her head on my chest. I'm trapped. There will
　therefore be a next time.

MAE
　He sneezes. He has trouble breathing.

LUDWIG
　I'm not feeling very well.

MAE
　Allergic to my handsome kittycat?

LUDWIG

I'm sick as a dog.

MAE

There won't be a cat "NEXT TIME."

LUDWIG

(*aside*) A nail in my coffin.

MAE

(*feigning surprise*) Oh! "Next time!" (*out of the game*) Aren't you glad I got rid of the cat?

LUDWIG

I should have guessed about the cat: you were covered in little white hairs.

MAE

That was the first weekend we spent together in bed.

LUDWIG

The first, yes.

MAE

It feels like we've been in bed ever since.

   Silence.

LUDWIG

We don't get along that badly.

MAE

Not when we're playing ... Tell me again about your first orgasm.

LUDWIG

The day of my first orgasm, God died of jealous convulsions. God, his buddies Satan, Apollo, Stalin, JFK, and the members of the World Wrestling Federation all died when the angels, archangels, the damned, and the saints joined me for a fine May afternoon to cheer me on. Something never before seen in all of history! They paraded along the adorable body of the girl in my arms. It made her laugh: hee hee hee. Me too: hahaha. Just before he died, the Devil peered over my shoulder and damned himself by looking down at her breasts ... Just before he gave up the ghost, Joe God in his divine person made himself tiny, then leapt onto my tongue, white beard, cane and all, and together we tasted the heavenly hatch ... I cried out inadvertently, and inadvertently slammed the little God against the wall. I'd have called 911 but I had other things on my mind! I was in ecstasy! Of course, that was on the inside—on the outside I was busy, concentrating hard ... I composed a requiem for my former self on the back, the belly, the buttocks, the arms, the legs, the lips of my lover. There was music everywhere! It was the month of May—the month of Mary, the month where man makes like the maples. I was that slimy serpent Mary protects us from, that slimy serpent she goes on trampling till the end of time. My lover was still panting when she asked me the fatal question: "Do you love me?" Crazy as a loon, I said "Yes! Yes, I love you!" She also asked me to marry her. Crazy as a loon, I agreed to marry her: every single day, if I had to. She could have asked me to build her a temple, I'd have built it with my bare hands—I was crazy as a loon. Crazy as a loon on the first warm day. I opened the windows wide. (*Orson Wellesian*) Out with the bad air ... in with the good ... God died as I flung open the window. My passion was springing to life!

Silence.

MAE

Marry *me*. (*A beat.*) Build *me* a temple. (*A beat.*) Have you lost your spring?

> *Silence. LUDWIG nestles his head between MAE's breasts. He caresses them as though he were a child.*

MAE

(*gently*) Talk to me.

LUDWIG

Again?

MAE

Yes, again, now, and always, forever and ever—

LUDWIG

What do you want me to say?

MAE

I want us to really talk, to stop telling each other ridiculous stories. We don't really know each other.

LUDWIG

We don't?

MAE

You don't know everything about me.

LUDWIG

I know you inside out—

MAE

Give me a break—

LUDWIG AND MAE

"That isn't a justifiable comment, it's even—"

LUDWIG
> (*finishing*) "Gratuitous."

MAE
> All right.

LUDWIG
> "All right then, I won't say another word."

> *A beat.*

MAE
> (*determined*) Talk to me!

LUDWIG
> (*grandiose*) "What we did on our trip to Baie Saint-Paul, by Ludwig Tessier. (*declaiming*) The sea lapped the shore of Baie Saint-Paul. It was grandiose! (*new declamation*) Foam washed the ship while the sky drooled on our sun-bleached heads. It was breathtaking! (*a third declamation*) Dusk enveloped us in its invigorating mist ... and we dried our bodies shadowed by our tender gestures. It was sublime!" (*stops playing*) Is that what you want to hear?

> *A beat. LUDWIG is confused: his sarcastic words have sounded almost beautiful.*

MAE
> You're romantic in spite of yourself.

LUDWIG
> Have you ever heard of parody?

MAE
> Have you ever heard of sublimation?

> *MAE tenderly massages LUDWIG.*

LUDWIG
Don't you ever get fed up?

MAE
Of what?

LUDWIG
Of giving.

MAE
I'm not fed up yet.

As though to prove it, she gently nuzzles his neck.

LUDWIG
Stop it!

MAE
Oh, now you don't like that?

LUDWIG
No! Uh ... yes, I like that ... But not now, especially not
now, not later, not ever ... I can't take it anymore ...
Stop!

MAE
Giving?

LUDWIG
Giving.

MAE
You're a coward.

LUDWIG
Yes.

MAE
Are you afraid of owing me?

LUDWIG
Maybe …

MAE
I don't give to get, Ludwig. I give out of love.

LUDWIG
But if I don't give back, you ask me what's wrong. You obsess about our relationship, you cry, you want to make love forever and always, and I don't know what I want to do.

MAE
You're not happy with me?

LUDWIG
I don't know anymore.

MAE
If you're happy?

LUDWIG
I don't know.

MAE
But you were once?

LUDWIG
I don't know.

MAE
With *her*?

LUDWIG
Who?

MAE
Your ex—the only one, it seems, that you loved.

LUDWIG
I don't know.

MAE
You don't know?

LUDWIG
I don't know anymore.

MAE
Maybe the problem is that I'm simply not her? I'm *like* her, but I'm not her exactly. Is that it? *She* was the death of God, but me, I'm *your* death, is that it?

LUDWIG
The way you talk about our relationship, I sound like an emotional ogre.

MAE
You never cease to impress me, Ludwig.

LUDWIG
(perverse) Do you want to be really impressed?

MAE
I really don't care.

LUDWIG
The story about my ex-girlfriend … I made it up.

MAE
You did not.

LUDWIG
I swear.

> *She takes this in.*

MAE
  Why?

LUDWIG
  To invent a past for myself.

MAE
  Are you toying with me?

LUDWIG
  Absolutely not.

MAE
  You weren't going out with that brown-eyed blonde four years ago?

LUDWIG
  No.

MAE
  Why did you keep bringing her up?

LUDWIG
  To stoke our passion?

MAE
  You're sick!

LUDWIG
  Maybe.

MAE
  Were you trying to make me jealous?

LUDWIG
  I don't know. Maybe.

MAE
  "Maybe, Maybe … " Are you done jerking me around?

LUDWIG

I don't know why I made up that story. I guess the brown-eyed blonde was *my* pregnancy scare.

MAE

Go to hell!

LUDWIG

What? Madam holds all the rights to fabrication?

MAE

I told you—(*disgusted*) Oh, I can't take it anymore!

Silence.

MAE

If I swallowed the story about your girlfriend, you must have fed me some other doozies.

LUDWIG

No no.

MAE

Really?

LUDWIG

I think.

MAE

What do you think?

LUDWIG

That's the only one I made up.

MAE

That's what you think?

LUDWIG

Yes.

MAE

So you lied to me about your past.

LUDWIG

What do you mean, "so." You're jumping to conclusions.

MAE

Am I wrong or not?

LUDWIG

You were wrong to put up with me for so long.

MAE

That's what I'm starting to think.

LUDWIG

But you were right to break up with me.

MAE

When?

LUDWIG

Last night.

MAE

Oh, you think this business is over? That we're really breaking up after coffee?

LUDWIG

That's what we said, isn't it?

MAE

You were half-asleep.

LUDWIG

Only half.

MAE

Do you take some kind of sadistic pleasure in tormenting me?

LUDWIG

No. Any other questions, commissioner?

MAE

What if I told you that before I met you I was perfectly happy, that when I saw you I felt sorry for you, that I thought you were pathetic, that I felt you needed both a mother and a girlfriend and I could be both, that I didn't want to feel responsible for, thus guilty about, your inevitable suicide?

LUDWIG

If you told me that, I'd believe you.

MAE

You're absolutely spineless.

LUDWIG

You're right.

MAE

What do you want from me?

LUDWIG

I want to be loved.

MAE

The way your fictitious ex-girlfriend would have loved you had she existed?

LUDWIG

I guess, yes.

MAE
> After I've drained myself dry to make our relationship work! What more do you want!

LUDWIG
> You're right, I'm pathetic.

MAE
> I feel sorry for you, Ludwig.

LUDWIG
> You probably do.

MAE
> Can you tell me what's keeping us together?

LUDWIG
> (*sardonic*) Love?

> *After a formidable silence:*

LUDWIG
> The baby—do you think—

MAE
> I really don't know.

LUDWIG
> But it's possible.

MAE
> It's possible.

LUDWIG
> Though you're not absolutely sure.

MAE
> No.

Silence.

LUDWIG

You know, no one ever said to me, "I love you."

MAE

That's the last straw! How many times have I said it, whispered it, shouted it?!

LUDWIG

Lots.

MAE

How can you drivel on that no one's ever told you that? Now he thinks he's Jean-Jacques Rousseau!

LUDWIG

Who?

MAE

It doesn't matter.

LUDWIG

No no, who?

MAE

"L'éternel incompris." A philosopher who claimed to be eternally misunderstood.

LUDWIG

Ah. Well, it's true, I *am* eternally misunderstood. I must take myself for Jean-Jacques whatshisface ... No one ever said they loved me before I met you. The first few times you told me, I was afraid. With time, I realized I was incapable of loving you perfectly, that I wasn't worthy of your love, or you. I'm a failure. I have a degree in Engineering that's totally useless; I've done a lot of reading, maybe a little too much ...

MAE

Oh, for Christ's sake. What have you read?

LUDWIG

I've read just enough to know too much, to realize I know just about nothing, to know that I'll always need to know more, but that I don't want to know more. Knowledge isolates you, but I already feel alienated enough from myself and everyone else. I've given up on humanity.

MAE

His Nibs has given up on humanity.

LUDWIG

I don't believe in myself anymore. You know, before you, no one ever said, "I love you" without expecting a caress or a kiss in return. No one ever said, "I love you" without wanting to hear it back. No one ever said, "I love you" freely—with no expectations. Even at home ... In our house we didn't say those sorts of things. We weren't very emotional in my family. A few generations ago the family decreed that no unreasonable emotions would be exhibited, that everything would be proper: repressed, hidden. It was more important to *appear* happy than to *be* happy. We were not to get carried away by any sort of tenderness, we were not to exceed the bounds of the platonic, of the rational. I saw both my brothers crying inside, sitting in front of the television. Hugo was miserable, so was Stefan. I'd have hugged them both, I'd have said to them, "I love you a lot." No, without the "a lot"—love is absolute, you don't need to amplify it. "I love you." But they'd have laughed at me. "Shut up," they'd have said, not wanting to miss a word the TV was spewing. They would have laughed at me, at my "faggy" impulses. A thirty-second commercial every ten minutes

isn't enough to build a relationship. I hate TV. I hate
commercials. I hate everything that cuts us off from each
other!

MAE
Ludwig …

MAE caresses him.

LUDWIG
Don't touch me!

MAE
Ludwig, I'm trying desperately to understand you, and it
still isn't working.

LUDWIG
There's nothing to understand.

MAE
I'm starting to despise you, Ludwig, and that scares me.

LUDWIG
You're right to despise me.

MAE
You're wallowing in your misery.

LUDWIG
In fictitious misery, to boot!

MAE
What's your point?

LUDWIG
(*smiling*) You know very well I don't have two brothers.

MAE
Yes, I know.

LUDWIG
> And you indulge my delusions? Why do you listen to me, Mae?

MAE
> Because there must be some truth in them.

LUDWIG
> If you say so.

> *A beat.*

LUDWIG
> I'd like to be alone.

> *A beat. She gets up to leave.*

LUDWIG
> Except I can't stay that way.

MAE
> Alone? (*LUDWIG nods. She continues, furious.*) What if I go out long enough for you to get your stories straight?

LUDWIG
> No.

MAE
> So, am I staying or leaving?

LUDWIG
> Stay, please.

> *MAE sits, far away from LUDWIG.*

LUDWIG
> "Stay." The neighbour used to say that with great affection: "Stay." Uncle Robert. Uncle Bobby. A neighbour. Bobby liked the neighbourhood children to

stay. It gave Robert a hard-on to see our little mouths so close to his belt. Big Bob liked to masturbate in front of us. Then, later on, *with* us, then later on, *inside* us. Mr. Robert Salin. The dirty bugger. I'm not making any of this up, I swear. Robert Salin … At least he didn't say, "I love you." All he ever said was, "Stay." And the kids would stay, the nice kids of the neighbourhood. "The Warriors," we nicknamed ourselves. The Brotherhood of Warriors. I remember the taste of his cock … Everyone would stay. And everyone would swallow … Then afterwards, everyone would go rinse their mouths out with Dumont's hose. We didn't talk about it. We never talked about it. Not even amongst ourselves, or to our parents. I don't know why, that's just how it was. After rinsing our mouths out at Dumont's, the Warriors went back to their children's games. *Our* children's games.

MAE

I didn't know.

LUDWIG

That we used to rinse our mouths out at Dumont's?

MAE

(*nervous laugh*) No.

LUDWIG

Dumont wasn't like Salin.

MAE

I hope not!

LUDWIG

Dumont LOVED us!

MAE

(*ready to leave*) Okay, that's enough melodrama.

LUDWIG

You don't believe me? It's true that Dumont really loved us! That's it, gent-ly, my boy. Gently, hold-it gent-ly … that's it. Ah! I love you, I love you!

Bitter laughter from LUDWIG. MAE stops—she remains stock-still.

LUDWIG

Actually, deep down I'm glad my parents never said "I love you." They must have loved me though—hypothetically, abstractly. I could love abstractly too. Maybe that's why I became an engineer. Devotee of geometrical passion. A lover of pure forms. Conical forms that swell with desire, that pierce that damp angle, the obtuse angle. Love is just something that swells—that rises up. Come here, come, my love, let me love you the way you deserve. Come! Listen: I love you!

MAE

No, not now.

LUDWIG

Do you hear me? I love you!

MAE

No!

He grips her, pins her to the floor, overpowers her. She manages to free herself. She moves away.

MAE

You fucking bastard! You scum! I don't give a fuck about your Dumont. Anyway, you lived in the country, far from all your neighbours, unless that was another tall tale. You want to hurt me? Go ahead, but don't beat around the bush! Don't try to soften me up, don't try to make me feel sorry for you because of your childhood scars.

She grabs his crotch and squeezes it.

MAE

Hit me! Are you looking for a rush? Hit me!

LUDWIG

No …

MAE

Hit me, pound me, strangle me if you have to!

LUDWIG

Mae! Mae. What's happening to us?

MAE

(*contemptuous*) You don't want to play anymore? You reject.

LUDWIG

I'm not a reject. My parents wanted me.

MAE

Are you sure? Did they ever say so?

LUDWIG

Shut up!

MAE

Did they ever say, "I love you"? I love you—that also means, "I wanted you, I still want you."

LUDWIG

(*crying*) Stop! What's happening to me?

MAE

(*imitating him*) "What's happening to me! TO ME: poor little me."

LUDWIG

You've made your point!

He bursts into tears. Silence. She calms down.

MAE

Ludwig …

LUDWIG

(*cold*) Don't talk to me. (*becoming enraged*) You're nothing but a leech. A vampire! A stain I can't get out!

MAE

You're scaring me.

LUDWIG

(*blind with rage*) Am I? You're scared of me? Do you want to be really scared!!?

> *LUDWIG grabs her by the neck, tears her pyjama top. He pushes her to the floor. As though preparing a missionary-style penetration. MAE breaks away.*

MAE

If you want to rape me, at least use the back door. You wouldn't want to ruin our chance of a little baby, huh?

> *LUDWIG is frozen.*

MAE

Go on! Shove it in, big guy, forget the KY, do your Salin. Do your Dumont. Be a MAN!

> *She sticks her ass in front of him, spreads her cheeks, arches her hips.*

MAE

(*screams*) Are you playing or not?

LUDWIG

I can't. I don't want to hurt you anymore.

> *Silence. MAE puts her pyjamas back on. They're afraid of each other.*

LUDWIG

We went pretty far, huh?

MAE

Yes … Too far.

> *Silence.*

LUDWIG

Mae, you know I'm not a *real* liar? I just can't tell you what I want, that's all.

MAE

I don't give a fuck!

> *Merciless silence.*

LUDWIG

I have a headache.

> *A beat.*

MAE

I feel sick. (*Silence.*) We have to go buy milk.

LUDWIG

For the coffee … (*Silence.*) Mae? (*A beat. She doesn't answer.*) I'm hungry. Unbearably hungry.

MAE
> So am I.

LUDWIG
> What do we do?

MAE
> We could eat?

LUDWIG
> Yes.

MAE .
> We could order Chinese food.

LUDWIG
> Yeah, Chinese.

MAE
> I'll call.

LUDWIG
> Yes.

> *Blackout.*

II

The Last Supper

*Lights up on the couple. The CHINESE DELIVERY GUY is
in bed with LUDWIG and MAE, sitting between them.
Under the covers.*

*All three are eating Chinese food with chopsticks and
all the rest. Laughter. Sexual tension.*

*MAE is acting the solicitous hostess, but underneath is
seething with bitterness and rage.*

*LUDWIG, despite his congenial front, is truly afraid of
losing MAE forever.*

DELIVERY GUY
No, really, I have to go …

MAE
Oh stay, please.

LUDWIG
We insist …

MAE
… and we're having so much fun.

LUDWIG
We haven't even had a chance to laugh at you yet.

DELIVERY GUY
Exactly.

MAE
Don't you feel good here with me?

DELIVERY GUY

Yes, yes. I'd stay if I could ... But I have deliveries
to make.

MAE

Your customers are getting hungry?

DELIVERY GUY

(*coining a maxim*) Those who wait are disinclined
to tip.

MAE

(*flirtatiously*) Don't you ever get hungry?

DELIVERY GUY

Me? Uh ... yes?

MAE

Hungry for adventure?

The DELIVERY GUY discreetly looks at LUDWIG.

LUDWIG

Don't look at me, I don't have a clue either!

MAE

Wouldn't you like to stay and talk to us awhile?

LUDWIG

Don't worry: we never do anything but talk.

DELIVERY GUY

With Chinese food delivery guys?

LUDWIG

There was a pizza delivery guy at one point ...

MAE

A handsome Italian who did his country proud.

LUDWIG
> Let's not get carried away.

MAE
> (*acid*) Because of course you never get carried away. (*to the DELIVERY GUY*) But you, my dear Chinese food delivery guy.

DELIVERY GUY
> What about me?

MAE
> Tell me a bit about yourself.

DELIVERY GUY
> I deliver Chinese food.

LUDWIG
> Really? You're kidding.

MAE
> (*to LUDWIG*) Don't you have a razor to sharpen?

DELIVERY GUY
> I have a stupid McJob, I don't have a girlfriend, I share an apartment with a roommate … oh yes, I studied Philosophy at University.

LUDWIG
> So you really hit the jackpot with this job!

MAE
> You can laugh your head off, Mr. Big-Shot Engineer. If it weren't for social assistance, you'd have stopped joking a long time ago.

DELIVERY GUY
> Oh, so you're an engineer?

LUDWIG

I studied mechanical engineering, I'm out of work, I sit on my ass, there's no room for me. I could have all the diplomas in the world … Anyway, you understand. Mae studied theatre, she makes people laugh, she's a crazy gal, and you studied philosophy and ended up delivering Chinese food. Well, we've covered everything: education, career plans, alternate sources of income. Let's move on to more serious things: like sex.

MAE

Ludwig!

LUDWIG

What? You don't feel like fucking our Chinese delivery guy? You don't have to pretend. I've seen it coming for the last hour. Go on, take his pants off, give him a blow job …

MAE

Don't worry, eventually I will, but you don't have to treat me like a slut. (*to the DELIVERY GUY, absolutely charming*) I'm sorry, he needs things spelled out for him. He's an idiot.

DELIVERY GUY

I understand.

LUDWIG

I understand that you understand! You've understood that she wants to fuck you, you felt it, you smelled her desire. You felt desire rise in you, you put a carton of fried rice over your desire; I saw you do it earlier. Listen, I'm not mad at you; I'm congratulating you. I'd have done the same thing.

DELIVERY GUY
You're talking as though I've slept with your girlfriend.

LUDWIG
She's not my girlfriend!

DELIVERY GUY
She's not?

LUDWIG
She's my *ex*-girlfriend.

A beat.

DELIVERY GUY
Oh. I see.

MAE
We broke up last night.

DELIVERY GUY
Ah. Anyone could tell.

A beat. LUDWIG scrutinizes the DELIVERY GUY.

LUDWIG
I like you.

DELIVERY GUY
Uh, thanks.

LUDWIG
We could be friends.

DELIVERY GUY
You never know.

Silence.

MAE

So that's it. We broke up last night. We're free!

DELIVERY GUY

The proof is you're still in bed together.

LUDWIG

(*ironic*) That's the greatest proof of freedom! Staying with your beloved, even when it's going badly.

MAE

Staying as long as it takes to enable the other person to leave—and in doing so, poisoning any hope of getting back together, while at the same time destroying whatever fond memories are left.

Silence. The DELIVERY GUY is uncomfortable.

LUDWIG

What were you thinking about when you wanted to fuck my ex?

DELIVERY GUY

I didn't—I mean, I wasn't thinking about …

MAE

It's pointless to argue, he's already got his talons in you.

LUDWIG

You weren't thinking of anything? Come on! I could see on your face that you wanted to—

MAE

Ludwig, you can see very well he doesn't feel like sharing his fantasies with you.

LUDWIG

And you, my darling, what were you thinking of?

MAE

> Don't call me your darling.

LUDWIG

> She's bitter! (*sweetly*) What were you thinking about?

MAE

> Nothing.

> *Silence. They wait.*

MAE

> It was a very simple—

LUDWIG

> Is that possible?

MAE

> Things are always simple when *you're* not involved.

> *Heavy silence.*

LUDWIG

> And the fantasy?

MAE

> It was nothing really, hardly even a daydream … I'm
> lying down … Billie Holiday is playing, there are candles
> all around; the Delivery Guy is in the bedroom, he's
> waiting for me to give him a sign. I nod, you come over
> to me, my dear Delivery Guy, you place a hand on my
> neck, the other on my shoulder, you kiss me, you lick me,
> you inhale me, you open my neck as though I were an
> oyster, you tickle me … And me? I laugh, softly, I tell
> you my fantasies; you, you savour the oyster, you don't
> hear a word of my fantasies, you aren't listening: you're
> acting them out. I tell you I imagine you're a woman and
> a woman entering me with your tongue that's parting my

lips, the woman you've become sucking my clit, and I shiver from your tongue darting between our lips. I get wetter than I've ever been in my life. You let yourself be swept away on the waves of our passion. I tell you I've finally come—for the first time in four years. But you continue, gently, between my neck and shoulder; your tongue is a song on my milk-white skin ...

DELIVERY GUY

The milk-white skin of a woman who's waited too long to be taken.

LUDWIG

Excuse me?

DELIVERY GUY

Nothing, I was embellishing.

MAE

He was saying he understood that I haven't been loved in a long time.

LUDWIG

(to the DELIVERY GUY) Is that true?

DELIVERY GUY

I don't know, it sounded good.

MAE

(disappointed) Thanks.

LUDWIG

Are you making fun of my girlfriend?

DELIVERY GUY

Don't you mean your ex?

LUDWIG

She might as well be my girlfriend. But, you're right.
My ex.

MAE

Since we've broken up for good.

DELIVERY GUY

Do you do this often?

MAE

Yes, every few months. We spend a weekend in bed
telling each other we're going to break up, we pull
outrageous scenes, and on Monday we're still here.
Except this time it's over for good.

A beat. The DELIVERY GUY is stunned.

DELIVERY GUY

I meant the games.

LUDWIG

What games?

DELIVERY GUY

Baring your souls, flirting with strangers …

LUDWIG

(*superficial*) What a coincidence, we were just talking
about that. Isn't that right, Mae?

MAE

(*glacial*) Yes, that's true, Ludwig dear.

LUDWIG

(*enraged*) Okay, that's enough! We're going to talk, once
and for all!

MAE

(*frosty*) Hearing you talk about our relationship, Ludwig, is like hearing a muffled Leonard Cohen song about the imminent death of a man who loves women too much, when we know he's been singing the same song for thirty years and the guy still hasn't died.

LUDWIG

Yeah, well I sing a lot better than Leonard Cohen!

MAE

(*continues, irritating him with references she knows he won't recognize*) Hearing you talk about our relationship is also like getting lost in an Escher staircase; it's putting your head in a hollow space sculpted by Anish Kapoor …

LUDWIG

Anish Kapoor! Where the hell did you get that?

MAE

(*ignoring him*) Hearing you talk about our relationship is like coming across the reflection of your ex-girlfriend in Velázquez's mirror; it's like reading all of Proust in one sitting; it's like trying to codify seduction based on a matrix of linear differential equations; it's like worshipping Beckett; it's like learning *Finnegans Wake* by heart; it's like dissecting a fly; it's like endlessly comparing loneliness and solitude; it's lecturing instead of living; it's understanding Sartre's *Nausea* because I've lived it every moment in your company; it's feeling the dagger of your faulty logic chop the little bit of feeling I had left for you into tiny pieces …

> *Silence.*

LUDWIG

So, shall I leave you two alone?

A beat.

DELIVERY GUY

(*getting up*) Oh, look at the time! I should check the meter.

LUDWIG

(*sits him down*) I WANT you to give yourselves to each other.

MAE

Just like that? Hop to it! In out in out in out. No flirting. No foreplay, no romance.

LUDWIG

Well, it's a carnal desire, without emotional ties.

MAE

What do you know?

LUDWIG

You want me to believe you love your Chinese Delivery Guy? (*to the DELIVERY GUY*) No offense, eh?

MAE

It's not only the act! *(to the DELIVERY GUY)* Right?

DELIVERY GUY

Uh ... the act?

LUDWIG

Come on. The act: sex, penetration, coitus, fucking. The act of giving it to her like there was no tomorrow!

DELIVERY GUY

I believe sexuality transcends the carnal act.

LUDWIG

> Watch out: our multifaceted Chinese Delivery Guy has decreed his catechism on sexuality!

DELIVERY GUY

> You start a debate but you don't even have the decency to follow through!

MAE

> The Delivery Guy is right.

LUDWIG

> Everyone's right except me.

> *A beat.*

MAE

> I have to go. I'll be back in a few minutes.

DELIVERY GUY

> I should go too.

LUDWIG

> To the washroom?

DELIVERY GUY

> To work. I've got deliveries to make—

MAE

> No, stay. Stay a while. I'll be right back. (*in his ear*) Don't leave me alone with him.

LUDWIG

> I'm sorry. I was a jerk, I can't help myself. Really, stay. I'd like us to talk.

MAE

> I'll be right back.

MAE leaves her men alone.

LUDWIG

So, you studied philosophy?

DELIVERY GUY

Uh, yes. For two years, then I dropped out.

LUDWIG

Oh. What a shame. (*MAE has left the room. LUDWIG changes his tone.*) Listen, I have something to ask you. You've noticed that we're a bit strange today? (*The DELIVERY GUY doesn't answer.*) You *have* noticed?

DELIVERY GUY

Yes.

LUDWIG

We broke up last night, except Mae would like us to stay together. Her little game is to convince me she doesn't need me. (*A beat.*) Are you following?

DELIVERY GUY

Yes, yes.

LUDWIG

So, don't take it too seriously, Okay?

DELIVERY GUY

Uh huh.

LUDWIG

Play the game, but don't get too involved. Mae is going to make you believe you're going to sleep together—or maybe she won't, maybe you'll simply develop a warm friendship, a deep bond. It doesn't matter, just don't get too involved.

DELIVERY GUY
    What if I don't feel like playing?

LUDWIG
    You'd have left a long time ago.

DELIVERY GUY
    What if our affections turn out to be genuine?

LUDWIG
    Hey! It's a game!

DELIVERY GUY
    For you, maybe …

LUDWIG
    It's a game for everybody, come on.

DELIVERY GUY
    Just for the sake of argument. What if I fell in love with
    her, and she with me?

LUDWIG
    Yoo-hoo! Is anybody home?

DELIVERY GUY
    Would you leave us in peace?

LUDWIG
    You really intend to seduce the ex-girlfriend right under
    her boyfriend's nose?

DELIVERY GUY
    Ex-boyfriend.

LUDWIG
    You've got nerve!

DELIVERY GUY
You insisted I stay.

LUDWIG
What I'm asking of you is very simple. She flirts with
you, you flirt with her: I pretend I find it cute; I leave you
to your business, she gets her kicks ... But if I find out
you've actually committed the act, I'll track you down
and I'll cut it off. Understood?

DELIVERY GUY
You're nuts.

LUDWIG
No; I'm just trying to avoid any misunderstanding.

DELIVERY GUY
You're always ready with a threat: you're a very small
man.

MAE enters, in a peignoir; LUDWIG improvises.

LUDWIG

"Threat of a small man." Ha! Ha! That's a good one! (*He
pretends he has just noticed MAE, and doesn't say a word
about the peignoir.*) Over to you, Mae.

MAE
What are you playing now?

LUDWIG
Instant definitions.

MAE
Oh. For what word?

LUDWIG

Erection. Our adoptive Chinese Delivery Guy has
defined erection as follows: threat of a small man. Good,
isn't it.

MAE

I'd say it's worrying.

Tense laughter.

MAE

My turn?

LUDWIG

Your turn! Ready? Erection:

MAE

Staff of life.

Same laughs.

LUDWIG

Over to you, my friend: Erection:

DELIVERY GUY

Uh …

LUDWIG

(*furious*) No hesitating!

MAE

Calm down, it's his first time … (*to the DELIVERY GUY*)
Are you ready? All right, one two three, erection:

DELIVERY GUY

Spontaneous salute.

MAE

That's a good one!

LUDWIG
You see, it's easy.

MAE
Idiot, it's your turn. Erection:

LUDWIG
(*macho*) Subtle as death!

MAE
Pfft.

DELIVERY GUY
No no no.

LUDWIG
Well, well. What a comeback.

DELIVERY GUY
Mae, your turn: Erection:

MAE
Sword of Damocles.

> *The DELIVERY GUY is impressed. MAE touches the DELIVERY GUY gently.*

MAE
You, my friend: erection:

DELIVERY GUY
Drawbridge of tenderness.

> *A beat.*

LUDWIG
That doesn't make any sense.

MAE
You don't think so?

DELIVERY GUY
Come on, it's a game.

LUDWIG
But a drawbridge goes down!

MAE
Will you shut up?!

LUDWIG
Will you excuse me for a few moments. I hear the
castrati singing.

> *One last vicious look at the DELIVERY GUY, then
> LUDWIG goes off towards those high voices.*

MAE
I hope our little frictions aren't annoying you?

DELIVERY GUY
Uh … no. I'm certainly not bored.

> *A beat.*

MAE
I'd like you to kiss me, tenderly.

DELIVERY GUY
Now?

MAE
Tenderly.

DELIVERY GUY
What about your ex?

MAE
No, he never kisses me tenderly.

DELIVERY GUY
Aren't you afraid he'll come in while we're—

MAE
He's already dead. He's on the verge of killing himself.

A beat.

DELIVERY GUY
Is he violent?

MAE
Yes.

DELIVERY GUY
The bastard! Did he hurt you?

MAE
Please, put your arms around me, kiss me gently.

He does so, too conscious of their proximity.

DELIVERY GUY
Is your boyfriend a psycho?

MAE
He hates losing. He hates not being in control. He doesn't know how to love, he doesn't love himself.

LUDWIG enters, carrying a piece of toast spread with Cheez Whiz. The DELIVERY GUY tries to extricate himself from MAE's embrace. She won't let him.

LUDWIG
Come on, don't be shy.

MAE

Ludwig, go away.

LUDWIG

What? Leave and miss the chance to live out my most repressed fantasy?

Silence. MAE and the DELIVERY GUY remain entwined.

LUDWIG

Don't you want to hear my fantasy?

MAE

No. Leave.

LUDWIG

(*too eloquent*) You, Mr. Chinese Delivery Guy with two years' education in philosophy, do you want me to leave? Do you want me to leave you with the woman who was my girlfriend until twenty-four hours ago? Shall I leave you, my happy little couple—the two of you together, in my bed—when if I leave you, I'll miss the perfect occasion to live out my fantasy?

DELIVERY GUY

What's your fantasy? Spit it out, let's get it over with!

LUDWIG

I really like you, we could be friends!

DELIVERY GUY

(*aggressive*) We'll see if that's what Fate has in store for us.

LUDWIG

I've always dreamed of seeing my girlfriend make love to a stranger.

MAE

> Do you want to know why?

DELIVERY GUY

> I'm sure he's going to tell us …

LUDWIG

> Because I'm a voyeur at heart.

MAE

> It's more that my ex-boyfriend is a premature ejaculator.

LUDWIG

> Have you finished beating up on me?

MAE

> He has no idea what a woman coming looks like.

DELIVERY GUY

> (*false candour*) Really? You poor thing.

> > *MAE snickers; the DELIVERY GUY bites his lip; LUDWIG becomes furious.*

LUDWIG

> All right, that's enough. Can I stay? Afterwards, I'll take off, I promise.

MAE

> (*to the DELIVERY GUY*) Do you feel like it?

DELIVERY GUY

> You?

MAE

> Since he's into suffering.

DELIVERY GUY

> You watch us make love, then you're out of here?

LUDWIG

Pfft. "Make love"—that's a lofty term for it. I'll leave after the act, *after* the female orgasm.

MAE

(*to the DELIVERY GUY*) I told you.

> *MAE begins the caresses, and the DELIVERY GUY gets into it. They kiss, fondle each other, nuzzle each other, desire each other, hold each other; this brings us to the moment of truth, the instant before penetration. Then LUDWIG remarks:*

LUDWIG

Oh, I forgot to mention … Mae's pregnant.

> *A beat. They stop. The DELIVERY GUY looks at MAE.*

MAE

(*embarrassed*) I might be, but it's not a problem.

> *The DELIVERY GUY gets up, horrified, and puts his clothes back on.*

DELIVERY GUY

I've had enough of your games! I'm getting the fuck out of here! You're both insane!

LUDWIG

Already? We haven't even had the chance to make fun of you!

> *The DELIVERY GUY is gone. Silence. The couple doesn't want to be alone. Absolutely not. Neither dares to look at the other.*

LUDWIG
It really wouldn't have bothered you to have him nail
you, even pregnant?

Silence.

MAE
(*disgusted*) I want my coffee.

A beat.

LUDWIG
There's no milk.

A beat.

MAE
True.

A beat. LUDWIG eats a bit of rice.

LUDWIG
Do you want some rice?

*Silence. LUDWIG moves towards MAE. He wants to hold
her, to caress her.*

MAE
(*acid*) Don't touch me.

*Silence. He moves away. They recoup their strength.
Blackout.*

III

The Cat, Victor, Returns from the War

Formidable silence.

LUDWIG

Mae, you know how much I need you. I really do lov—

Victor the cat returns after four years away. He enters the room, meowing, if possible.

MAE

Victor, you've come back!

She picks up Victor, pets him, holds onto him for the rest of the play.

LUDWIG

Look, the cat came back—what a coincidence! Victor the fleabag-allergy-cocktail-pain-in-the-ass.

A beat. MAE is comforted; she ignores LUDWIG who stands and paces.

LUDWIG

Mae, please, forgive me. I lov—

The DELIVERY GUY enters.

DELIVERY GUY

All right, listen. I've thought it over.

LUDWIG

Congratulations!

DELIVERY GUY
You, shut up! If I understood correctly, the two of you broke up last night.

LUDWIG
We did make that clear.

DELIVERY GUY
Are you going to let me finish?

LUDWIG
Of course. Do you want some coffee?

DELIVERY GUY
Uh, sure.

LUDWIG
We're out of milk, though.

DELIVERY GUY
That's fine. I don't take milk.

LUDWIG
Come in the kitchen. (*to MAE*) Your "boyfriend" came back, do you want coffee?

She ignores him, or doesn't hear.

DELIVERY GUY
(*gently, to MAE*) I'm back, I'll fix everything.

MAE hasn't heard a thing. LUDWIG and the DELIVERY GUY go into the kitchen. Or, a deus ex machina kitchen descends from the sky like a divine tray. LUDWIG makes coffee during the following.

LUDWIG
So, you've thought it over. Let's hear.

DELIVERY GUY

I ran away before ... I didn't get it ... But afterwards, it was perfectly clear.

LUDWIG

(*sardonic*) Perfectly clear?

DELIVERY GUY

(*lucid*) Yes. You want to break up but you can't bring yourselves to do it. Deep down you still love her and it makes you jealous that she's attracted to me—that there's chemistry between us ...

LUDWIG

You think?

DELIVERY GUY

I'm uncommonly perceptive ...

LUDWIG

It's true that to deliver Chinese food it takes—

DELIVERY GUY

Have you finished making fun of me?

LUDWIG

Actually, I'm almost done.

DELIVERY GUY

(*oh so candid*) Mae told me you treat her like shit. I won't tolerate you seeing her. I love her. I wouldn't let anyone treat her badly for anything in the world!

LUDWIG

(*incredulous*) What planet are you from? You love her. (*He snaps his fingers.*) Just like that. You saw her, you love her. I already hear wedding bells.

DELIVERY GUY
 I want you out of her life.

LUDWIG
 That's what you want?

DELIVERY GUY
 She begged me not to leave her alone with you.

LUDWIG
 (*amused*) Go on, this is getting interesting!

DELIVERY GUY
 What do you mean, go on?

LUDWIG
 Oh. You're finished?

DELIVERY GUY
 Yes. I'm staying, you're leaving. I'll take care of Mae.

 Silence. LUDWIG scrutinizes the DELIVERY GUY with a sardonic smile. He no longer has a monopoly on disdain. The coffeemaker is boiling; the coffee's ready. LUDWIG makes two cups.

LUDWIG
 You really amuse me. I'm sure we would have become great friends.

DELIVERY GUY
 Will we ever know?

LUDWIG
 Surely not. Go take Mae her coffee. Here's yours.

DELIVERY GUY
 (*still just as serious*) I'm going to talk to her.

LUDWIG

> I hope so!

> > *LUDWIG wipes the counter while the DELIVERY GUY takes MAE her coffee. She doesn't notice either the DELIVERY GUY or the coffee.*

DELIVERY GUY

> I came back, just like I promised! Here's your coffee. (*A beat. MAE doesn't react.*) Drink, you look like you need it.

MAE

> (*not understanding a thing*) Who are you?

DELIVERY GUY

> Come on, it's m—

LUDWIG

> (*enters, falsely joyful*) So, all is well? Is the coffee to your taste? Perfect. I'll leave you two now. I have to go; you understand, the cat, my allergies, and I might get in your new suitor's way … And it's so lovely outside … I think I'll go kill myself. Don't worry about me, it'll be a beautiful death. Painful, bloody, lonely. Like the guy said: "To be, is to be trapped." (*a little fake laugh*) Adieu.

DELIVERY GUY

> That's right, bye, see you around.

> > *LUDWIG exits through the kitchen.*

DELIVERY GUY

> Go on, have your coffee.

> > *She takes it, robot-like.*

DELIVERY GUY

Do you need anything? (*A beat.*) Do you want to talk? (*A beat.*) I just realized—you don't even know my name! It's Al—

MAE

(*cutting him off, without looking at him*) I don't want to know.

A beat. The DELIVERY GUY's *mouth hangs open—he's incredulous.*

DELIVERY GUY

(*playing psychologist*) I understand. You don't feel like talking.

MAE

What are you doing in my bed?

DELIVERY GUY

I've come back! I came back to take care of you.

MAE

Go away. (*Silence. The stunned* DELIVERY GUY *doesn't move.* MAE *insists.*) Get out of here!

DELIVERY GUY

Mae, I love you!

MAE

(*placid, observing*) Did you hear that, Victor? The Chinese delivery guy has known me less than a day but he loves me! And to think I wasted so much time with a monster! Ludwig'll have to die alone; I don't have the strength to die too. I can't feel guilty anymore. (*MAE looks at the* DELIVERY GUY.) There isn't even any milk in my coffee. Do you realize that? There isn't any milk!

DELIVERY GUY
(*uncomfortable*) You're right, what was I thinking? Coffee without milk is such a—

MAE
Leave me alone, please. Victor's comehome.

The DELIVERY GUY leaves. MAE keeps on petting Victor. Slow blackout.

APOCALYPSE

or

The Magnificent Curtain Call of an Ordinary Everyday Ludwig

—A ceremony—

(Rappel)

Rappel was first produced on May 12, 1995 at the National Arts Centre Studio in Ottawa by Théâtre la Catapulte in collaboration with Animatics Multimedia Corporation and the National Arts Centre. The play was directed and designed by the author. Cast and crew were as follows:

FIRST MOUTH /
UNCANNILY NUBILE ANGEL . . . . Valérie Cantin
SECOND MOUTH. . . . . Isabelle Bélisle
THIRD MOUTH /
UNCANNILY NUBILE ANGEL . . . . Dominique Allard
AN ORDINARY, EVERYDAY LUDWIG. . André Perrier
A GIACOMETTI-STYLE COW
. . . . Sasha Dominique Normand
YET ANOTHER POPE. . . . . Mario Gendron
A DETHRONED MUSE . . . . Isabelle Bélisle
LUDWIG'S DYING FATHER . . . . Marc Bertrand
A DRIFTING MAE . . . . Chantal Aubut
A CHINESE DELIVERY GUY SADDLED WITH
A TOO-COMMON NAME . . . . . . Simon Garneau
UNCANNILY NUBILE ANGEL. . . . . Maxime Turcotte
Designers: . . . Animatics Multimedia, Geoff Levine,
. . . . Tracy Alves, Joël Beddows,
. . . . Christian Sénéchal
Technical Directors: . . . . Cathy Mitchell,
. . . . Phillip Whiteside, Joël Beddows,
. . . . Christian Sénéchal

This English version of *Apocalypse* was read in May 2009 at Playwrights' Workshop Montreal.

Cast (in order of appearance):

ONSTAGE CHARACTERS:

Three Mouths.
An ordinary, everyday Ludwig
Yet another Pope.
Ludwig's dethroned Muse.
A Giacometti-style Cow.
An uncannily nubile Angel Choir.

OFFSTAGE VOICES:

Mae adrift.
Chinese Delivery Guy saddled with a too-common name.
Ludwig's dying father.

PLACE:

In Ludwig's bachelor apartment. But especially, in Ludwig's imagination.

TIME:

The play takes place over the course of a few weeks, chronologically. There is no need for any convention to mark the passage of time.

STRUCTURE:

Stream-of-consciousness: fluid, anarchic, sexual, but also rhythmic, visually dynamic, cyclical.

The soul that cries out for social life cries, not because it is permeated with social feeling, but because this feeling is lacking.

—Rudolf Steiner

An impetuous and disordered dilettante in everything I do, I will have only truly known one thing: the inconvenience of having been born.

—E. M. Cioran

A 3-D MOUTH with full lips is projected onto a screen.

FIRST MOUTH
> (*rhythmically*) Wanting, wanting to feel fine, to feel fine,
> to drink wine, this wine of oblivion, letting it trickle in a
> thin stream, a red stream, red like lips, these red lips,
> these full lips receiving the thin stream, the red stream,
> thick parted red lips, wanting, wanting another set of
> lips, wanting another, wanting company, keeping
> company, parting company, being apart, being alone,
> feeling, alone, alone again, wanting, wanting to feel
> fine …

A SECOND MOUTH appears.

SECOND MOUTH
> Wanting …

FIRST MOUTH
> To drink …

SECOND MOUTH
> Wanting to drink …

FIRST MOUTH
> To see past the drink …

SECOND MOUTH
> Yes, to drink, drink this wine …

FIRST MOUTH
> No more wine …

SECOND MOUTH
To drink this wine of oblivion …

FIRST MOUTH
The wine's gone …

SECOND MOUTH
Trickling in a thin stream …

FIRST MOUTH
Oh no, the stream's run dry …

SECOND MOUTH
Dried up for good …

FIRST MOUTH
I'll never drink this wine again …

SECOND MOUTH
Drying up …

A THIRD MOUTH appears.

THIRD MOUTH
Fingering the stream, caressing it …

SECOND MOUTH
Dried up …

Spotlight on the straight razor in LUDWIG's hand. We make out LUDWIG's unmoving shape but do not see his face.

LUDWIG
It was lovely out. The sun was absolutely glorious. I had just made coffee for Mae and her new boyfriend, a certain Chinese delivery guy. There was no milk for the coffee.

SECOND MOUTH
> Drinking, thinking, drinking black coffee …

FIRST MOUTH
> Drinking black coffee, always black, black coffee …

THIRD MOUTH
> With open pores, open to black coffee …

SECOND MOUTH
> Black, the red bleeds black, from black coffee …

THIRD MOUTH
> Pores and taste buds always tasting, and the coffee
> flows …

SECOND MOUTH
> No, the wine flows …

FIRST MOUTH
> No more wine ever …

THIRD MOUTH
> And the coffee pours, the throat roars, rrrrraaahh!

SECOND MOUTH
> RRRRRRRAAAAAHH!

LUDWIG
> Victor the cat had just come back after a four-year
> absence. The entire duration of my relationship with
> Mae. I had to leave, to keep myself from hurting them,
> Mae, the delivery guy, the cat.

FIRST MOUTH
> Nothing left to do but drink coffee and ruminate on
> what makes us tick, life ticking away, *briiing*, waking up

to life, coffee and life and the pained liver and heart, oh the heart …

THIRD MOUTH

The heart, oh yes, beating hard, ba-boom, ba-boom, the heart, oh the heart, and coffee, and her absence …

SECOND MOUTH

My head's spinning …

FIRST MOUTH

My heart's racing …

SECOND MOUTH

Yes, my heart, my heart and coffee …

FIRST MOUTH

Trying to wake up, trying to cheer up, looking for the crowd, looking for company …

SECOND MOUTH

The companionship of the crowd …

THIRD MOUTH

The anonymous crowd …

LUDWIG

I shut the door gently behind me. I walked for a long time. I even remember I was whistling an old Marlene Dietrich tune. I couldn't remember the words. I also remember the deep blue haze that descended on me, the grinding sound and the sparks of the razor being sharpened.

FIRST MOUTH

The crowd, coffee and the heart, the little heart, flee, flee from the heart, the little heart, the crowd, those lips, that smile ... I'm smitten, flee, flee from it. (*The lips continue to chant flee, flee from it while LUDWIG finishes his diatribe.*)

LUDWIG

(*losing his cool, still not moving*) The more I walked, the bluer it was, the harder it was to see, the foggier it was, the angrier I got, the deeper I sank, sinking into darkness. There was still this razor being sharpened on the grindstone. (*He imitates the sound.*) I found a little corner, crawled up into a hole, a crevasse, behind a vulture's nest perched high up on a cliff. I rush towards that cliff, towards the crevasse, the hole. I'm finally alone! Staring my death in the face.

> *Black, with a spotlight on the answering machine. The blinking light reveals that there are several messages. The lights come up slowly. LUDWIG'S PERSONAL MUSE is there, dressed in black leather, like a dominatrix. She's knitting a long scarf: ten or fifteen metres at least. A POPE is playing chess against himself, lying on his belly on the floor. A GIACOMETTI-STYLE COW is centre stage, a bit closer to the back.*

COW

Ludwig, you've got messages.

> *Silence. LUDWIG hasn't heard.*

COW

Ludwig, you've got messages.

> *LUDWIG isn't listening.*

COW

Ludwig, you've got messages.

MUSE

(*looking up from her knitting for a moment*) All right already, Cow! We heard!

COW

Ludwig …

LUDWIG

(*annoyed*) What do you want?

COW

Don't you want to listen to your messages?

LUDWIG

(*indifferent*) No.

COW

(*impatient*) Hey Pope, play the messages.

POPE

Why?

COW

Because I'm bored.

POPE

Things are nice and quiet here for once.

LUDWIG

(*irritated*) Why do you two always have to talk and talk and talk?

COW

I'm bored.

POPE

The Cow wants us to listen to the messages.

LUDWIG

(*indifferent*) Fine, sure, if you want …

COW

Go ahead, Pope …

POPE

(*still playing chess*) I'm busy. I've almost won my thirtieth consecutive game. Can't the Muse do it? Hey, Muse!

MUSE

(*dressed in black, knitting*) Knit one, purl two, knit one … forty-eight. (*irritated, to the* POPE) What?!

POPE

Go play the messages on the answering machine.

MUSE

Go yourself, you've got legs!

POPE

A man can't get any respect here anymore! Why do I have to do everything? Why would your Pope suddenly turn into everyone's personal minion? I've got more important things to do! You'll see, one day I'll issue an edict and you'll have to respect me!

COW

(*cutting him off*) Shut up, Pope!

> *The* POPE *gets up, grumpy. Presses the button on the answering machine, sits down.*

FATHER'S VOICE

Ludwig? Are you there? Yoo-hoo! I know you don't always pick up, even when you're home … (*He waits for* LUDWIG *to pick up.*) All right. I guess you're out. So, it's your dad …

MUSE
Yeah, we figured that much out.

FATHER'S VOICE
How's it going, kiddo?

COW
(*to the answering machine*) He can't say.

FATHER'S VOICE
Listen, I figured I'd invite myself over for supper on
Tuesday. What do you think? I'll bring the wine. Call
me.

Answering machine beeps.

POPE
Tuesday, that was the day before yesterday.

Second message.

FATHER'S VOICE
Ludwig? Hello? Hello? Are you there, kiddo? I haven't
been home, so if you called, I'm sorry, but you know,
Some things are beyond our control, destiny sometimes
gets in the way. So listen … I can't come over for supper
tonight because I've just met the most gorgeous … Oh
man! You should see her! She must be about eighteen!
(*Laughs.*) Okay, so I'm exaggerating a bit. Well, call me,
we'll have breakfast and compare STDs. (*Laughs.*)

MUSE
The swine!

LUDWIG
That he is.

Answering machine beeps.

MAE'S VOICE
> I'm at the airport, Ludwig. At the gate. I'm leaving soon. I just wanted to hear your voice. I'm leaving, on a trip. I'll call again …

> *Answering machine beeps. Everyone looks at LUDWIG; he looks sad.*

CHINESE DELIVERY GUY'S VOICE
> Oh … I think I finally have the right number! If this is Ludwig Tessier's number … um … well … I'd like you to … I'd like him to call me back. Ludwig. You … um … he knows me. It's Alain. Alain Lalonde, the Chinese delivery guy from the other day. Remember me? I slept with your girlfriend, you watched us, and then just before I entered her, you told me she was pregnant. Right. It's a bit weird to put it so baldly … Anyway, your girlfriend … I mean your ex-girlfriend … I mean … You know what I mean … Mae left a basket outside my door the other day. It was Victor, the cat, and there was a note. She wrote that she was going on a trip and that I should take care of the cat. I just thought that maybe, you know, you wanted it, you know, the cat … Anyway, call me back. Oh yeah, I'm at 557-9798. Bye.

> *Answering machine beeps.*

COW
> Hey, dumbass. Ludwig is allergic to cats.

> *Next message.*

CHINESE DELIVERY GUY'S VOICE
> Hey. It's me again, it's Alain.

POPE
> Alain?

CHINESE DELIVERY GUY'S VOICE
Alain Lalonde.

POPE
Alain Lalonde?

CHINESE DELIVERY GUY'S VOICE
The Chinese delivery guy.

POPE
Oh, it's you.

CHINESE DELIVERY GUY'S VOICE
Yeah, it's me. You know … Remember what I said yesterday, about you taking back your cat? You know, Victor?

POPE
(*to the others*) Get to the point!

CHINESE DELIVERY GUY'S VOICE
It's just that … Okay. You see, Victor the cat just got hit by a truck. I'm sorry. I'm really really sorry. I'll buy you another one. I'll call back later.

Answering machine beeps.

POPE
Maybe you should call back and tell him that you were allergic to the cat, that you always hated that cat, and that you're actually quite happy he's dead.

LUDWIG
(*smiling, passive*) I should …

Pause.

POPE

Are you going to let him suffer? The poor guy'll be worried.

LUDWIG

Yes.

POPE

You have no heart! Whatever happened to your sense of Christian—

LUDWIG

Leave me alone! (*The phone rings. LUDWIG flies into a rage.*) Leave me the fuck alone! (*The answering machine picks up: "Hello, you have reached ... etc."*) Turn it down, I don't want to hear him.

MUSE

What if it's Mae? You should talk to her, Ludwig.

LUDWIG

Turn it down!!!

POPE

(*Turns down the volume of the answering machine, so the message is inaudible.*) I just know it's that poor Chinese delivery guy ...

LUDWIG

(*turning to him menacingly*) You're starting to piss me off!

POPE

You can't just leave him like that ...

LUDWIG

Shut up!

POPE

No, I don't want to shut up. I am expressing a serious concern!

COW

Why don't you mime whatever you want to express; then we can just shut our eyes, and you can express your head off.

POPE

I don't want to be a stupid mime; I don't want to play charades; I want to be heard; I want to be listened to! Listen to me!

MUSE

(*sarcastically*) Go on, you can do it, express yourself!

COW

Relax, calm down, okay? "What's your name?"

LUDWIG

No way, you're not playing that game!

POPE

"My name is … Alain Lalonde."

LUDWIG

Your name is not Alain Lalonde!

COW

Oh yes, we're playing; we're playing!

MUSE

(*putting her knitting down*) "Alain Lalonde? That's a nice name. Alain Lalonde. Did you know, Alain Lalonde, that you are an absolutely unique individual?"

The answering machine beeps, the message is over.
LUDWIG gives up. He lets the characters in his mind
throw themselves into the game.

POPE

"An absolutely unique individual?"

COW

"Unique, Al! Why don't you tell us a bit about yourself.
Why did you come here today, Al?"

POPE

"I just came, just to listen, I don't really have anything to
say."

COW

(*authoritative*) "Al, we know you have problems, you have
to talk them through!"

MUSE

"Concentrate. Take your time. You can do it, Al, we're
here to listen."

POPE

(*concentrates, takes his time, realizes he can do it*) "Hello.
My name is Alain Lalonde, and I wanted to grow up to
be a philosopher."

COW AND MUSE

"Go on, Al, you can do it, we love you!"

POPE

"I wanted to be a philosopher, but there's not really any
future in philosophy. The only way to survive in the field
of philosophy is to be a professor, and to be a professor,
you have to mutate into an academic, and to fully mutate
you have to be able to reason according to systems of
philosophical analysis, and to really reason properly, you

have to kill the seed of madness known as irrationality, and to really wipe out that seed, you have to structure your thinking in a Cartesian manner, and to be linear and scholarly, you have to deny everything magical or strange, and once you've suppressed everything strange, your thinking will never be original again, and without delinquent thought, all that's left for you is to teach, all you can do is entertain your students with sophisms, and endlessly define inductive and deductive reasoning, and have your masturbatory thoughts funded by the Academy. I didn't have it in me to become a professor. But I couldn't imagine myself thinking full-time and not actually making money from it. So I got a job delivering Chinese food.

MUSE
"Hey, that takes guts, delivering Chinese food."

COW
"I used to know an art historian who would do anything to be in your shoes, Al."

POPE
"Oh yeah? Why's that?"

COW
"Because on top of his Masters in art history and his other Masters in comparative international political science, he had the misfortune to take, just by chance, an introductory course in gerontology."

POPE AND MUSE
"Oh no! Not Intro to Gerontology!"

COW
"Alas, yes. Everyone thought he should take care of the elderly; because they said old folks are the future. The

future will be all about taking care of the past, making sure it stays clear and present."

POPE

"In the end I'm really glad to have the privilege of delivering Chinese food. This way, I get to travel, I meet people, I make a bit of money. I don't have to ask for hand-outs from our glorious and exemplary nation. I can really say I'm a model citizen, proud of putting my talents for delivery and interpersonal communication at the service of our public good. I don't have to worry too much either. No one likes people who worry too much. They're annoying, they ask too many questions. Chinese delivery guys? They're like kids fresh out of school, they exist to serve the dominant class and patiently wait for their tips. I like my job, and I'm not a failure."

COW AND MUSE

"Way to go. Thanks for sharing that! We respect you for what you've become."

POPE

"Am I one of you now?"

COW AND MUSE

"Yes! Yes! You are, you're part of a generational proletariat. You have a position, even if it's a McJob. We respect you for what you've become."

MUSE

"You may now respond to the accusations of the good and decent folk."

COW

Here, I'll play one of the good and decent folk. Ready? Okay: "Lazy bum, all you have to do is get a job!"

MUSE AND POPE

(*bowing at COW's feet*) "Please excuse my impertinence, your grace, but I do have a job, I've even shelved the aspirations my generation was raised with to serve you better, I've even squelched my intelligence to serve you better. I have a position, bent over before you!"

POPE

(*vacuous and blissful*) "I'm finally happy."

ALL (*except LUDWIG*)

(*rubbing their stomachs*) "We are finally happy. Yum. Yum. Yum."

LUDWIG

Fuck you, Alain Lalonde.

> *Pause.*

COW

Come on Ludwig, just because you don't like him, you don't have to be uncouth. We're not in a bar, you know.

LUDWIG

(*still angry, but playing along nevertheless*) "You're a sell-out, Lalonde! Fuck you!"

MUSE

He wants a bar? We'll give him a bar.

POPE

A bar! I'll be the bartender! I can give advice to the poor disillusioned souls; I know every whore in town ...

> *The lighting and sound turns into the bar.*

MUSE

> (*to POPE*) Let me. (*She walks towards LUDWIG, feigning shyness.*) "Hey there ... I'm Alain ... Alain Lalonde ... I'm here with you tonight to get over my shyness. My doctor told me to write or act or sing or take courses in basket weaving or something to get over my shyness, so I made up this song to sing to you tonight. (*oh so fake*) Here's a little ditty I just wrote yesterday. (*to the musicians*) Okay, ready boys? (*announces*) 'The Eternal Loser Country Blues.'"

> *The musicians play "The Eternal Loser Country Blues" with a lot of twang.*

MUSE

> I laugh even when I didn't get the joke
> No one notices me, but all I want is to be like other folk
> I keep on smiling 'cause beggars can't be choosers

CHORUS

> I'm a piece of crap, I'm the king of losers.

MUSE

> Girls run to me when their boyfriends make them blue
> I stroke their hair and I hold them, hoping for my chance to woo
> But each one goes back to a guy who'll only use her

CHORUS

> They don't stay with me 'cause I'm the king of losers.

MUSE

> Couples sometimes let me join them for kinky stuff
> I film them but when my turn comes, they've suddenly had enough

CHORUS

I put up with shit, 'cause beggars can't be choosers
I'm a piece of crap, I'm the king of losers.

MUSE

I try to get drunk and drown my pain in beer
But the barman looks right through me, it's like I'm not
even here

CHORUS

I put up with shit, 'cause beggars can't be choosers
I'm a piece of crap, I'm the king of losers.

LUDWIG

"Fuck you, Lalonde!"

COW

"Go deliver some pizza!"

MUSE

(*kindly intervening*) "Actually … it's Chinese food."

POPE

"You're fuck all, Lalonde!"

LUDWIG

(*getting into the game*) "Lalonde! You came on to my girlfriend, asshole! I saw you talking to her the other day!"

POPE

"It's true, I saw him talking to her too. He grabbed
her ass!"

COW

"He didn't just grab her ass, he bent her over and fucked
her brains out, I saw him. He told me 'this is how to fuck
a jerkoff's girl.'"

LUDWIG

"You shithead. I'll get you for that! No one touches my girl. No one!"

POPE

(*laughing*) "Not even you, it seems."

LUDWIG

(*looking daggers at him*) "I'll deal with you later."

COW

(*maliciously*) "Plus, I heard that Lalonde smacked your girl around."

LUDWIG

(*seeing red*) You hit my girl?! (*grabs the* MUSE) You hit my girl?!

MUSE

(*pleading*) "No, it's not true. I never even talked to her … "

POPE

"Yeah, he smacked her around and then he laughed about it!"

LUDWIG

"You laughed? You shithead! (*hits the* MUSE) You don't hit women!"

MUSE

(*cynically*) Sure, buddy. Beat up your own conscience.

LUDWIG

(*hitting the* MUSE) "You don't hit women!"

MUSE

(*cynically*) That's right. Beat up your own conscience.

LUDWIG

(*still hitting the* MUSE) "You don't hit—"

POPE

(*moving towards* LUDWIG) Whoa! Whoa! Ludwig, you're
going to hurt her!

LUDWIG

(*still in his role*) "Fuck off, take your hands off me, are you
a fag? You don't want me to destroy your precious little
Lalonde?"

POPE

(*firmly, not playing*) Ludwig, that's enough.

LUDWIG

(*far gone now*) "Oh! Now I get it! You're a Lalonde as
well! (*to the* COW) And you too, you little weiner, you're a
Lalonde too. I knew it! You guys, you Lalondes, you stick
together. You love each other so much that you even
marry each other! You love each other so much that you
ass-fuck each other! I know you Lalondes! When you're
not fucking each other, you're sticking it in the calves.
That's why you stink so much! Insane fucking family!
Smacking around other people's girls! You shitheads! I'm
gonna fucking kill you all! I'm gonna exterminate you,
one by one!"

> *The phone rings. Everything stops. The* MUSE *motions
> to the* POPE *to turn up the answering machine. The*
> POPE *does so. The message:*

MAE'S VOICE

I'm lost, Ludwig. I'm at the heart of a labyrinth, I don't
know where I am, it's swallowed me up, I can't find my
way out. How long before the Minotaur arrives? Am I
the virgin-muse?

MUSE

(*interrupting*) Hey, I'm the muse!

POPE

(*pondering*) We raped her a long time ago, the virgin-muse …

LUDWIG

Shut up!

MAE'S VOICE

And when will Morpheus take me? And when will death come? Ludwig, I'm afraid. There's nothing left. Nothing. The sky here is decadent. It smells like peanuts and honey. All the tourists, there are too many tourists, each stupider than the next. Everyone's yelling, there's too much yelling, and there's too much junk for sale that's way too expensive. I'm in the heart of the labyrinth, and these con-men are trying to tell me it's New York. I'm in the middle of a tumour, a cancer. Too much life. There's too much life here, Ludwig. All this excess makes me dizzy, puts me on edge. The excess of humanity evokes death. The acrid breath of death. Death smells like life's excess, Ludwig! Nothing makes sense. I've been circling the city for days: the Upper West Side, Spanish Harlem, Central Park, Fifth Avenue, Chinatown, Alphabet City, the Lower East Side, Wall Street, the Harbors, Columbus Circle, Broadway, Greenwich Village, Soho … It's a closed spiral, Ludwig. I have to get out of here, just to keep from imploding. I have to live, survive. I can't die here. I don't want to be the virgin in the heart of the labyrinth; I'm leaving. Somewhere else. I'll call again …

Answering machine beeps.

LUDWIG

The virgin in the heart of the labyrinth! And she used to accuse me of turning everything into allegory!

POPE

And yet you must acknowledge your predilection for weirdness and excess.

LUDWIG

What do you mean?

POPE

Your imagination. Mind you I'm not unhappy to be part of it, but think about it: A Muse and a Pope living in your subconscious mind?

COW

What am I, chopped liver?

POPE

Oh yeah, I forgot! A cow! And a scrawny cow at that!

LUDWIG

What's wrong with the cow? You don't like the cow? I like it, I like that cow a lot! (*to the COW*) Cow, I'm very fond of you.

COW

(*tenderly*) Thanks, I'm fond of you too, Ludwig.

LUDWIG

See? There's nothing wrong with a guy having a cow in his head, a cow that he's very fond of, especially when the feeling is mutual!

POPE

(*impatient*) Okay, fine, everyone should make room in their head for a nice cuddly cow. But what about your

whore of a muse? And what about me, your
omnipotent Pope?

LUDWIG

An omnipotent Pope? Don't go overboard! You merely
represent the spiritual and the sexual.

POPE

Spiritual and sexual, sure, that's fine for me, but what
about the Muse?

LUDWIG

She embodies the spiritual and the sexual as well.

MUSE

(*knitting*) Me? All I've done for four years—maybe even
longer—is knit. I can't think any more ... And as for the
sexual, it's all dried up down there. And to tell you the
truth, I was never into it.

COW

You were never into it!?

MUSE

Not really.

COW

You were never into it!?

MUSE

Maybe a little, but not anymore.

COW

You were never into it!?

MUSE

All right, all right! Yes, I liked it. I loved it; I was crazy
for it! For me, sex represented fertility. My sexuality fed

all of Ludwig's desires, all his ideas and insights. But ever since Ludwig started ignoring me, ever since he forgot about me ...

LUDWIG
Come on, I think about you often.

POPE
The proof is you're still here! Lucky for you that he thinks about you; if it were up to me, I'd have had you drawn and quartered long ago.

MUSE
Back in the day, no one would dare say, "Hey, Muse!" I was respected. I was envied, and desired, too ...

COW
Hah! "Desired" might be a bit strong ...

MUSE
No! I know that you desired me. You too, you little fart!

POPE
(*truthfully*) Only when I masturbate. Er, masturbat*ed*.

MUSE
Back in the day, I didn't sit around wasting time with you losers. Ludwig, you'd summon me, you'd summon the Muses and I played them all for you. With a flick of the wrist I became Clio, Muse of history. I liquefied into a sea so that you could dive into me, soak me up, splash around in the collective memory. You wanted to dance? You wanted to move, to finally inhabit your body? With a hop I metamorphosed into Terpsichore, Muse of dance. Once you were present in your body, you wanted to master it, to see how it resonated, what it could sound like ... you wanted to sing. So you summoned me by the

name of Polymnia, Muse of sacred music, and I showed you how to give voice to songs that let you soar up to the clouds. And I accompanied you, as Euterpe, on the flute. Then your song became profane; you wanted to use your reason, to debate. And I was still there except that I became Calliope, Muse of eloquence. But it wasn't enough to know how to speak; you had to speak with intelligence and talent. So I contracted into a ball of fire and settled beneath your sternum, I became Thalia, Muse of comedy. And then things got complicated, and fate stepped in. To save you from being manipulated by the gods and the hypocrites, I protected you like a guardian angel, I turned into Melpomene, Muse of tragedy. You cursed the gods, you raised your fist to the heavens; you vowed to understand the world so you could avoid any more unpleasant surprises. You summoned the Muse of astrology, and when I arrived, you asked me, "Urania, what should I do?" And my answer was: "become an engineer." You studied forms, mathematical functions, physics, but it wasn't enough. Now you needed to be emotional, sexual, erotic. You liked me well enough back then. I became Erato. But you didn't like that name. You called me only "She." You liked to say, "She comes back to me like the chorus of a song, a never-ending song." You constantly delayed my arrival so that you could enjoy anticipating my presence. You went crazy as soon as I opened my mouth. You always wanted more. You declared eternal love and faithfulness to me. You told me that the other women in your life were nothing to you, that I was the only one that mattered, that you looked for me in other women's faces, that you saw me in other women's eyes, that you could pick up my scent in a crowd, that the sight of a rainbow would fill you with my taste … You adored me, Ludwig. You adored your own idea of love. You turned

me into love incarnate, so that you could, some day,
easily extract me from love itself. Then you realized that
you'd been so caught up in your crazy illusions that you
didn't see me for what I was and you started respecting
me. You discovered that I had a voice, that I was realer
than real, that I had ideas and instincts, that I could hold
my own, that I could easily put you in your place,
question you, provoke you. Then, one day, you didn't
want anything from me. You didn't summon me anymore
for my charms, you didn't ask me for ideas. You didn't
seek me out anymore. You felt guilty. You tried to force
yourself to see me, at least a few times. You always asked
me to play. But I had exhausted the entire pantheon of
muses, all that was left was for me to be the virgin-muse.
The fleeting muse. And you perverted me, you raped me,
you wanted me to like it, you dressed me in leather and
then you could no longer stand my presence. Seeing your
inspiration looking like a whore … and now? I knit! I
comfort you and I knit!

POPE
That's not true!

COW
That's not true!

LUDWIG
That's not true!

MUSE
What's not true?

POPE
Your story!

COW
Your story.

LUDWIG

Your story.

MUSE

I knit. I comfort you and I knit!

POPE

I saw you sewing the other day!

COW

I saw you stirring an imaginary pot!

LUDWIG

I never raped you!

MUSE

You traded me for despair. You looked at me and
announced: "Here's my inspiration, I'll put it in a plastic
bag, just like a piece of dog shit when you take your mutt
out for a walk. My inspiration, the very marrow of my
being, a piece of dog shit." Woof, woof, I'm a dog. Oh,
look, there goes a beautiful woman. Woof, woof, hello,
hello, I'm panting, my ears are pricked up. And there
goes the shadow of a doubt, there it goes. Woof, woof, I
got it, I'm playing dead, my four little paws in the air.
There goes a vague perception of death, that way. Woof,
woof, I growl and growl, no one will come near me any
more. Oh, there goes the angel of despair, woof, woof,
I'm an animal, a submissive animal. Hey, there's another
one, and there goes another one, and look, there's
another one woof, woof, woof, woof!

LUDWIG

That's enough!

MUSE

(*faking submission*) What? You want me to go back to my knitting? (*Pause.*) There goes the garbage truck, there it goes! Woof, woof, oh yes, oh yes! I love that smell! Oh yes, oh yes! I love to bark! And there goes the razor, right there, straight to the neck, straight to my neck, cold metal blade!

COW

That was unnecessary!

POPE

A little restraint, if you please!

LUDWIG

All I can see is my impending death.

MUSE

And yet, I'm still knitting. I'm knitting you a bandage, a really nice bandage. Woof woof!

COW

That's enough with the dog!

MUSE

That's all that's left in your head—a dog's dreams!

POPE

I object! I'm still here! And I'm worth more than a dog's dream!

LUDWIG

(*confused*) I can still tell stories, like I used to …

COW

I was just going to ask you to tell us a story, like you used to. Something to set this poor rambling Muse straight.

MUSE

(*feeling ganged up on*) Be my guest!

LUDWIG

(*carried away*) Okay, come on, let's do "The Fable of
Neighbour Salin Who Loved Too Much, and His
Sidekick, Neighbour Dumont, Who Always Asked
for Seconds"!

POPE

(*serious and worried*) But fables are supposed to be about
animals, not humans. I'm sorry Ludwig, but a rule is a rule.

LUDWIG

You don't want fables?

COW

Sure, we can do a different fable. One featuring cows,
perhaps?

LUDWIG

If you won't let me do fables, I'll have to present you
with "The Sad Story of Neighbour Salin Who Loved
Too Much, and His Sidekick, Neighbour Dumont, Who
Always Asked for Seconds." Because, you know,
neighbour Salin loved too much and his buddy,
neighbour Dumont, always asked for seconds. This must
be the most tragic and the most comic postmodern
tragicomedy ...

MUSE

Ludwig, we don't like that story!

LUDWIG

What?! You think it's too tragic? Too comic? At least you
can't accuse me of lacking inspiration!

MUSE

I don't think we should laugh about it, Ludwig.

LUDWIG

We have to laugh about it; it's the only way to get even. Contempt and irony are our weapons!

POPE

It's just us here, Ludwig, you don't need to defend yourself.

COW

You're just rubbing salt in the wound.

LUDWIG

(*not listening*) Neighbour Salin, you know, he loved us, he loved us all, all of us brave little neighbourhood kids, the Brotherhood of Warriors! After he initiated us to the facts of life, neighbour Salin made his rounds with a bulge in his pants. (*too cheerfully*) Neighbour Salin headed off, whistling, la la la la la, dear old Uncle Salin. "Good day, Mrs. Tessier, how are you today? Well?" "Oh, I'm very well, couldn't be better." "Your tomato plants are looking very healthy!" Doo-di-doo-di-doo. Dirty old Uncle Salin whistling, going to visit neighbour Dumont. He knew the Warriors too. Neighbour Dumont also thought we were a lot of fun. Ha ha ha ha! He thought we were a riot. "Oh yes, do the cow again, do the calf. Ha ha ha ha! Don't move a muscle, I'll get the camera, we'll have a laugh later! Robert, help him with his underwear, the little dear. That's right, take them off. Oh! What a darling little penis. Do the cow! (*singing*) And the cow jumped over the moon ... "

COW

(*sadly*) You shouldn't, Ludwig.

LUDWIG

(*seeing red, mounts the* COW) Yes, I should! Think of posterity! It's not enough to be creative, you have to record your work! Being creative isn't enough—you have to archive your work. Yes, I should! Do the cow! Moo! Moo!

> *The* MUSE *and the* POPE *pull* LUDWIG *off of the* COW. *They struggle.*

LUDWIG

(*as neighbour Dumont*) Let go of me! Hey! "I'll teach you to use your claws, you little snotface. Robert, catch him!"

POPE

(*to the* MUSE) Play the mother!

MUSE

The mother?! Ludwig's mother?

POPE

Play the mother, for Christ's sake!

MUSE

(*as* LUDWIG's *mother*) "Hello there, Mr. Dumont. Oh!? You seem to be a touch out of sorts."

LUDWIG

(*startled*) "Uh ... no. I just lost my little cow."

MUSE

"Your little cow. Ha ha ha! Have you been drinking again? You devil, you! Anyways, your wife is looking for you, she's at our place. We're making jam: rhubarb, strawberry, raspberry, currant ... "

> *The phone rings.* LUDWIG *snaps out of it, falls down. The* MUSE *and the others all breathe a bit more easily.*

FATHER'S VOICE
(*electropop music in the background*) Hello. Hello? Yoo-
hoo! I know you're there!!

LUDWIG
(*sneering*) Ah, my hero.

FATHER'S VOICE
Aren't you ever there?! I forgot: my son is a free man
again! Are you out chasing skirts, kiddo? Well, I'm at the
club, and I think the girls are getting younger and
younger! Not that I'm complaining! Ha ha ha ha! So ... I
feel a bit awkward ... but you know, I met a really hot—
and very respectable—young lady here, tonight, and as it
turns out, she's not alone. She's got a friend with her, and
well, since you've been alone for a few weeks now, so I
thought maybe you'd like to come down ... You never
liked going out with your old dad, did you? Don't worry,
these young ladies are legal, they swore they were! You
should see them! They're the cutest things. They're fresh!
Not like the others. The others here reek of desperation.
Everyone reeks of desperation. Myself included, I'm sure.
Everyone's dancing, everyone's drinking, everyone's on
the prowl. So much desperation. No one talks here. You
can't hear anything over the music anyways. People talk
through their eyes and their bodies. Even when girls
don't look at you, you can tell if they're interested by
looking at their hands. So many available hands. More
hands than glances, I'd say. I like it better that way. We
recognize each other without looking, we get to know
each other without much talking. I like it better that way.
A heartbroken man is silent, for fear of seeming
pathetic ...

LUDWIG (*laconically*) AND FATHER'S VOICE (*strongly*)
"A man who is alone and useless is pathetic."

LUDWIG

How many times? How many times have you used that little gem?

FATHER'S VOICE

Oh! My friends are back … Don't worry about me, I'll take precautions. I won't make the same mistake twice! Anyways, I'll be here at the club if you want to come join us. It could be a fun family outing! Ciao.

Answering machine beeps.

LUDWIG

(*through clenched teeth*) What's stopping me from killing him?

POPE

The fear of falling into cliché.

LUDWIG

What cliché?

POPE

The Freudian myth in which every son wants to kill his father.

LUDWIG

I want to make up my own myths.

POPE

That's what's stopping you from killing him.

The phone rings.

LUDWIG

(*yelling at his father*) Now what do you want … to do it in my bed?

MAE'S VOICE
Hey. You're never there.

LUDWIG
(*listening, lost*) Mae ...

MAE'S VOICE
You're never there. Me neither, I'm not there anymore I
think, I don't know anymore. I'm starting to think like
you: all I need is a little space ... Did you know that
Sartre lived in this hotel? Simone de Beauvoir too, in
another room. I learned that today. Oh, yeah, I'm calling
from Paris, you aren't here, neither am I really, nor am I
with you. I don't know why I'm calling you. So why am
I? Did you know about Sartre and de Beauvoir? I didn't.
I went to the cemetery where Jim Morrison is buried. It's
pathetic. There was graffiti everywhere. Jim's head.
Flowers. The graffiti will fade, the flowers will wilt, and
the fans will die just like Jim. Nothing endures. I'll call
again, from somewhere else ...

> *Answering machine beeps. Pause.*

LUDWIG
(*sucker-punched, but not emotional*) Realizing that she's
not there anymore. Imploding, collapsing into myself.
Noticing a circle of waves surrounding me, rolling
towards me ... Feeling a very moist lament rising up.
Squeezing my eyelids shut. Squeezing them tight.
Wringing and Extracting. Everything. Flowing. *The
Birth of Liquid Anguish*. An outgrowth. Cancer. Excessive
life is parasitic. Multiplying. I have a cancer growing
right here. A cancer eating away at me. Too much ...

> *Pause. Everyone looks at LUDWIG without saying a
> word. LUDWIG changes his tone. The grindstone suddenly
> starts up. A column of light illuminates it from above.*

LUDWIG

Let's get things cleaned up! Cow?

COW

Yes, Ludwig?

LUDWIG

You're going to put my thoughts in order.

COW

That's no small task! (*She gets to it anyway.*)

LUDWIG

(*not listening*) Muse. You're going to research effective suicide methods.

MUSE

Chinese water torture!

POPE

What's the matter with you?!

MUSE

A turpentine-soaked guillotine!

LUDWIG

Never mind, I'll do it myself. You can tidy up instead.

MUSE

You asked me for ideas, I gave you ideas but you don't want them! Honestly, you're always making me play either the mother or the nymph! What's a personal Muse if she's not a mother or a nymph?! (*She gets to work anyway.*)

LUDWIG

(*not listening*) Pope?

POPE
Ready!

LUDWIG
Take notes.

POPE
(*resigned*) Fine, sure, I'm used to it. (*Sits down with a pen and paper.*)

LUDWIG
Cow, are you done?

COW
Don't rush me! I'm still on the anecdote of dirty old Robert Salin.

LUDWIG
That sick fuck!

POPE
(*writing it down*) Noted: "sick fuck."

LUDWIG
(*annoyed*) Not right away!

POPE
You should have said so.

COW
Ludwig?

LUDWIG
Yeah?

COW
I'm having trouble telling the true from the false.

LUDWIG

If you thought of it, it's true.

COW

So what's false?

LUDWIG

Anything you can't think of.

COW

What am I supposed to do with that?

LUDWIG

You'll figure it out. My dear Pope, are you taking notes?

POPE

Oh, so now you want me to write.

LUDWIG

(*Dictating his will.*) "In the event of my premature death, I leave my apartment to the first comer, who, like me, can't afford to live anywhere other than this dump; I leave my place in the welfare line to the first comer who, like me, wasted time in university under the illusion that the world would be waiting for him when he graduated; I leave my bike to the first comer so that he can enjoy a brush with death every time he gets on it; I leave the lock to the first comer so that he can hit the crazy drivers where it hurts them most: their cars; I leave my books to the bureaucrats and senior officials so that they can know almost as much as their employees fresh out of graduate school, who do all their most important photocopying; I leave my mismatched furniture to the couch potatoes of another era who constantly want to relive their younger days; I leave these twelve test tubes of my sperm so that my time here will have meaning, so that twelve little terrorists will keep the adults, the rich and the beautiful from fucking them over; I leave my CD collection to anyone in need of escapism; I leave my little national-but-only-in-the-eyes-of-some flag to the anthropologists; I leave everything that I have an extra one of at my mom's house to the next victim of shared custody; I leave my computer and modem to the first comer looking for friendship and communication; I leave my brain to Science, for the distraction of a few medical students looking for laughs; I leave my mutilated anus to necrophiliac undertakers: may they get gangrene; I am not leaving whatever is left in my bank account to anyone, that way the government will be forced to manage my frozen money, it will cost them double what it's worth in administration fees and it will never circulate again, my way of thumbing my nose at the new religion: the economy. The new religion of those who, in their youth, were Maoists, Marxist-Leninists, communists—believing themselves to be original thinkers but really masters of ideological plagiarism. I leave my contempt for all that is false, especially society; I'm not leaving any declarations of love, because I never learned how to love; I'm not leaving my soul, because it's the only thing that ever really belonged to me.

"I don't want a religious ceremony, or to be buried in a cemetery, or to be mourned. Leave my naked body in a public space—at the shopping mall—with a sign around my neck that reads: *This heretic did not believe in the Economy, or in perpetual youth for adults, or in the future, or in himself. He mutilated himself, trying to shock us. Applaud him for his courage in sparing us his wrath.*"

Pause.

LUDWIG
Did you get it all?

POPE

It's a bit long. These days, if you can't distill everything into sound bites …

COW

We could always put cowbells around his neck.

POPE

No! He needs a sign worthy of him, like that other guy had, you know, Jesus.

MUSE

We can write: "*Antidemocratic heretic: killed himself because he had nothing better to do.*"

POPE

Perfect!

COW

It's not cowbells, but it'll do.

LUDWIG

It'll make me seem like an insignificant little whiner!

POPE

Isn't that what you want?

LUDWIG

No! I want society to look bad, not me.

POPE

According to Erikson—

MUSE

We don't give a shit about Erikson!

POPE

No, but listen … Erikson wrote: "*I am what survives of me.*"

COW

So if you come across as a failure, as a young man full of potential but who never had a chance to succeed, it's not your fault!

MUSE

Except that if we are what survives of us, Ludwig doesn't amount to much …

COW

The test tubes!

MUSE

What, you want to make the same mistake as our parents? Make peace, make love, make babies, then abandon them, then whine all your life about how much it costs to have kids, real estate is a better deal …

POPE

(*for LUDWIG*) You can't just leave the test tubes and hope that someone will use them; you have to take responsibility.

MUSE

(*for LUDWIG*) Yes! We have to survive! If only to prove that we can.

COW

(*for LUDWIG*) We have to survive, we have to live, if we want to fix what's broken.

MUSE

(*tenderly*) Do you really want to die, Ludwig?

LUDWIG

(*fiercely*) You won't make me change my mind!

COW

Have you seriously thought this through?

LUDWIG

I don't want to hear it! (*to the POPE*) The suicide note.

MUSE

We won't let you die, Ludwig. (*changing her tone*) I changed from Muse to mother without you even noticing.

POPE

(*offended*) What the hell is going on in your head?

COW

You think we're over the top?

MUSE

(*frivolously*) My little tuft of hair tickling your nose …

POPE

Maybe you'd be living in a cozy apartment if it hadn't been for the Bauhaus's influence on modern architecture.

COW

It's my moral duty to be vegetarian.

LUDWIG

(*holding his head in his hands*) How can I make this craziness stop?!

POPE

You can't imagine what will become of you?

MUSE

You can't choose what to wear tomorrow?

COW
> You can't think what cut of meat to get at the butcher's tomorrow?

MUSE AND COW
> You can't undo the part of you that died at birth?

MUSE, COW AND POPE
> You can't decide to live? You can't tie your own shoelaces? You can't tie a Windsor knot? You can't manage to fold your top sheet back to the standard forty-five degrees? You can't keep an erection when you masturbate? You can't remember how your mother's lips used to pucker just before she kissed you? You can't remember the songs that you sang at Scout camp? You can't imagine who will come to your funeral, or even less, who will mourn you? You can't remember the rule of seven?

MUSE
> Don't you trust us anymore, Ludwig?

LUDWIG
> My head is spinning.

COW
> Don't worry, Ludwig, we're just bouncing ideas around.

LUDWIG
> I'm plagued by madness!

POPE
> (*indignant*) Don't go overboard, she's only knitting.

MUSE
> I wouldn't mind doing something else, but you know, Ludwig isn't interested.

LUDWIG

I'm a piece of shit.

POPE

(*mocking*) Too true.

COW

(*mocking*) Without the shadow of a doubt.

MUSE

(*mocking*) A mistake.

LUDWIG

No! I wasn't a mistake!

MUSE

Yes you were. Didn't your father just say, "I won't make the same mistake twice"?

LUDWIG

It's not true! It's not true! It's not true!

POPE

(*robotically, emotionless, continuing under the next few lines*) Oh dear, I hurt, oh dear me, pain pain pain ... (*etc.*)

MUSE

Has anyone ever said, "I love you"? "I love you" also means, "I wanted you, I still want you."

LUDWIG

I'm not reliving that scene.

COW

(*sarcastically*) Has anyone ever told you, "your birth was the high point of my existence"?

POPE

Holy cow!

LUDWIG
> It's not going to work.

COW
> What if we showered you with utterly gratuitous and insignificant insults?

POPE
> Yes! I'll start!

COW
> I wasn't announcing the next game, I was asking him a question.

POPE
> (*to LUDWIG*) Half-baked smegma face!

COW
> Pope! We're not playing!

POPE
> (*to the COW*) Second-rate David Cassidy!

COW
> That's enough!

MUSE
> (*to the COW*) Mosquito-shit!

COW
> (*to everyone*) Lice-infested butt crack!

POPE
> (*to the MUSE*) Anorexic fagstration!

MUSE
> (*to the POPE*) Syphilitic tonsils!

COW

I'd even call him a diptheria-dicked chauvinist!

POPE

(*to the COW*) Voltaire-spouting turd!

COW

(*to the POPE*) Pedophile.

MUSE

(*to the POPE*) Mutilated ectoplasm!

POPE

(*to his two aggressors*) Omnifunctional Serbo-Hungarian prototypes!

COW

(*to the POPE*) Disillusioned piece of estrogen!

MUSE

(*Second take. Insults the COW.*) Rectal wart!

COW

(*to the MUSE*) Piss-stained linoleum chewer!

POPE

(*to the MUSE*) Fascist piece of manure.

MUSE

(*to the POPE*) Crab-brained zealot!

POPE

(*to the MUSE*) Undying skankiness!

COW

(*to the MUSE*) Bellybutton breath!

MUSE

(*to the COW*) Passive-aggressive fudge-packer.

POPE

(*to the COW*) Rectangularly regal rictus.

COW

Bloody puddings!

POPE

(*to the COW*) Cheesehead.

MUSE

(*to the COW*) Ingrown toenail.

COW

(*to both*) Necrobiological parasites!

POPE

(*to the COW*) Mummified mime.

MUSE

(*screaming*) Transcendental fart!

COW

(*screaming*) Crystallized herbivore!

POPE

(*screaming*) Screeching amoeba!

> *Exhausted, they burst into laughter, fall down.*

POPE

Now that was fun!

> *During the tirade, LUDWIG has reread the suicide note. Silence. Then everyone remembers LUDWIG, looks at him.*

COW

What don't you want to tell us, Ludwig?

LUDWIG

(*fiercely*) Nothing. I want to clear my head.

POPE

(*incredulous*) Are we preventing you from clearing your head?

Pause.

MUSE

What aren't you saying, Ludwig?

LUDWIG

(*bitter*) What aren't I saying? I'm not saying "toodeloo," I'm not saying "fraud." I'm not saying "antidisestablishmentarianism," and as far as I know, I've never, ever deliberately said "the cow jumped over the moon."

COW

Thanks Ludwig, I'm just fine right here.

LUDWIG

You see?

COW

And you? Ludwig, are you fine?

LUDWIG

No I'm not. I can't make you shut up!

POPE

Oh, well, you know, Ludwig, that's impossible! As long as you're alive, we'll be on your mind, in a manner of speaking.

LUDWIG

We can fix that. Quick: suicide methods!

MUSE

You could slice your jugular …

POPE

Or, you could start by dismembering your Muse.

MUSE

Goddamned Pope!

POPE

(*sourly*) His Holiness, my dear personal Muse.

> *The MUSE goes to LUDWIG, tries to seduce him. They grope each other, breathe each other in …*

COW

Hey, don't blaspheme, Pope. That's *Ludwig's* muse.

POPE

A Muse is a Muse.

COW

Ludwig's personal Muse isn't available to just anyone.

POPE

Well, since he's turned her into a whore …

COW

And he calls himself a man of God, a man of the Holy Spirit!

POPE

He's turned her into a whore!

COW

Ludwig only turned his Muse into a whore because he didn't have the courage or the strength to feed his inspiration. She'll always be his personal Muse; she'll always belong to his imagination. Even as a whore, she's still his personal muse.

POPE

I say that when a man makes his personal Muse into a whore, it means that his Muse is effectively a whore.

COW

So Ludwig is his inspiration's pimp?

POPE

Inspiration is a commodity, my dear bovine, and you can barter it just like talent, and vocation, and …

MUSE

(*annoyed by these incessant stupid remarks*) Do you plan to keep this up for long?

POPE

We're having an important theological discussion.

MUSE

Jesus Christ! A cow and this poor excuse for a pope are having an important theological discussion!

COW

Yes! Maybe Ludwig could help us resolve the issue …

LUDWIG

Resolve what issue?

POPE

Our theological issue.

LUDWIG

Your theological issue! Ooh, that's serious! I can tell you that I know for a fact, I know in the very marrow of my bones: yes, one hundred thousand angels can dance on the head of a pin.

The phone rings.

MUSE
It's God!

MAE'S VOICE
Gneixendorf, Ludwig. The axe falls, the axe chops. Gneixendorf, Ludwig. Gneixendorf. Beethoven stayed here. As in Ludwig van. In Gneixendorf. I've been thinking of you, of us, of Beethoven, of what we were to each other before everything got too complicated in our little heads … I'll call again.

Pause.

LUDWIG
(*nostalgic*) Have I already told you how, four years ago …

POPE
(*uninterested*) … you were so handsome …

COW
(*just as uninterested*) … you screwed like rabbits …

POPE
(*mocking*) … you blasted Beethoven so loud …

COW
(*mocking*) … you opened the curtains of the window facing the street so wide …

MUSE
Enough, you guys. Drop it! This isn't the time!

LUDWIG
I disgust myself …

COW

> (*pokerfaced*) You disgust us too.

> *The COW and the POPE have a good laugh.*

LUDWIG

> I've had enough!

> *LUDWIG rolls back the carpet on the floor, revealing a chasm that belches flames and smoke.*

COW

> Whoa, whoa! You can't just get rid of me like that! It was a joke!

LUDWIG

> I've lost my sense of humour.

COW

> I am an intrinsic part of your imagination. If you get rid of your Cow, all equilibrium will be lost! You'll have no more moral milk for your coffee of existence. Can you imagine your Pope without your scrawny Cow? Who is he going to discuss theological matters with? Your Muse?

POPE

> You know, every since I read Leander's *Treatise On the Education of Virgins*, the Muse and I can't seem to talk theology anymore.

COW

> Ludwig, you don't want to lose your equilibrium, you know how fragile you are, keep me close to you …

MUSE

> (*cynical*) … and keep your enemies closer.

LUDWIG

(*calm, determined*) Enough of these games.

> *The grindstone starts up; a bathtub descends from the heavens. It's a religious moment for LUDWIG because it's part of the ceremony LUDWIG desires. The POPE goes to get the razor, sharpens it. The lighting is focused on the POPE's actions. While the POPE sharpens the razor, LUDWIG takes off his clothes, gets into the bathtub, covers his body with shaving cream. The MUSE joins him, cuts his hair. He dunks his head under the water; then the MUSE covers it with shaving cream as well. The POPE goes to the bathtub and gives the MUSE the razor; she shaves LUDWIG's entire body while the POPE, now in the pulpit, recites his "Treatise on Violence and its Necessary Implosion."*

POPE

"On Violence and its Necessary Implosion."

"Doing violence to oneself without restraint requires the inexorable determination of the dying man who accepts his imminent death.

"The violent being gives himself over to the demanding lover that is death.

"The civilized soul acknowledges that violence must not be repressed, but that it must be channelled inward, towards the self.

"The necessary implosion of violence is motivated by an altruistic concern for maintaining a healthy tension of the social fabric.

"Violent personality types:

"The primitive personality exhibits uncontrolled violence. His violence is physical and savage, directed towards children, women, the elderly.

"The primitive who has been instilled with some moral values is only violent with strangers, and only on occasion. He seeks occasions.

"The repressed primitive will use verbal abuse, defamation, conspiracy.

"The professional primitive personality revels in channelled violence, he is found in the military or the government.

"The intermediate personality, believing himself to respect others, inflicts violence solely on his own person. He is characterized by low self-esteem, psychosomatic ailments, alcohol and drug abuse, self-mutilation ... By doing violence to himself the intermediate personality makes life unbearable for those around him.

"The advanced intermediate personality will undertake a minutely, almost clinically calculated self-destruction. He will take great pains to not disturb others."

The MUSE is still shaving LUDWIG.

POPE

(*continuing*) "The advanced violent personality practices intellectual violence on himself. He probes his own depths in search of perpetual provocation. No rest for this type who is always working towards his own demise.

"Finally, the fully realized violent personality dives into the heart of the poisonous torrent, knowing full well that in the battle against death, the only way to win is to choose one's own time."

The phone rings. The purification ritual continues, no one pays attention to the message.

CHINESE DELIVERY GUY'S VOICE
Uh … Hello? Okay, so this is another message for
Ludwig. It's Alain Lalonde. I've called a couple times
already, about the cat. Victor the cat. Anyways, the cat is
dead and all that, and I bought another one, a real nice
one. A purebred. It cost a fortune. I know I should've
waited for you to call. I don't even know if you're there,
or if this is even the right number … Anyways, if this is
Ludwig's place, and if you ever happen to listen to your
messages, I got you another cat, a purebred, but it was
also hit by a truck … I can't take it anymore … It seems
like I'm no good at anything. I feel like the ultimate
loser. Anyways, whatever. It's been fabulous talking to
your answering machine. Bye.

> *Answering machine beeps. The MUSE is still shaving
> LUDWIG. The POPE and the COW watch.*

MUSE
The ocean-man sinks down into himself, he caresses
himself freely, playfully, lewdly.
The ocean-man opens his mouth, descends to the lower
depths, these ocean depths that he recognizes as his own.
The ocean-man comforts himself, opens his pores, lets
the sea in; he is a sponge.
The ocean-man tastes himself, the saltiness, finds him-
self too blue, observes himself from these depths. He's so
blue, so blue.
He rocks, he is lulled by the waves:
Me
     Me
        Me
           Me
              Me …

The COW, the MUSE, and the POPE repeat, sometimes in harmony, sometimes dissonant, the wave's word: "Me." The phone rings. The audible wave continues.

MAE'S VOICE

Ludwig? I'm in Brittany! I like it here. I'm in a region where people choose to be. Not only are they born Bretons, one day they declare their Breton identity loud and strong, without being forced by flag, law, and anthem, and even while another flag, law, and anthem are forced on them. Three hundred thousand people marched from here, Ludwig, in the Chouan uprising. In 1793, the peasants and the petty nobles rose up against Paris. They refused to be conscripted, they refused to give up their livestock, they demanded freedom of religion, and really, just more freedom in general. Here, people believe. I don't know what they believe in. But they believe. Ludwig, I think I'm happy here. I really think so. I'll call again.

Answering machine beeps. The "Me" waves are still audible, in celtic harmony. The phone rings again.

FATHER'S VOICE

(*embarrassed*) Hello? Ludwig? Are you there? (*Pause. The "Me" harmonies stop.*) It's your father … Listen, I really need to talk to you. It's been a while since we talked, eh? We never talk anymore. Not because I don't call, mind you. (*Breathes hard. He's having trouble.*) I want us to talk, Ludwig … (*Angry.*) How come you never return my calls! You don't want to talk to me anymore, is that why? Are you ashamed? Ashamed of your old dad? You're ashamed that your old dad is still so young? What's your problem? You have everything you need! For Christ's sake, you have everything! You have your life ahead of you! Your life! I did everything to make sure you young people would have your lives ahead of you. I did it all twenty years ago, and now you're ruining everything. You're making us old, you're making us responsible.

LUDWIG

(*rushes at the answering machine*) Fuck you, Alain Lalonde!

The MUSE and the POPE hold him back, calm him down. He lies down naked on the floor.

FATHER'S VOICE

You were right not to come to the club the other night. Remember, when I left you that message, I was with two young women, girls your age … Why aren't you there?! Listen … I have to talk to you, I'm afraid you won't call me back … that you'll never call back. You know they laughed at me? They laughed at me! I bought them shooters all night and we were all feeling each other up, and then the brunette—the other one was blonde— asked me for a fifty; I gave it to her, like that, no questions asked, I wanted her so badly; the brunette disappeared, and the blonde and I went outside, we sat down, she started giving me a hand-job through my pants. Then a group of punks came by to harass us. One of them called me "gramps," another said that his buddies were ass-fucking my wife while I was messing around with the blonde. I got pissed off, I got up, she laughed, the punks laughed too, then the brunette came back and held me back, she took us both by the hand and brought us to her place. The three of us, can you believe it! They undressed me, the brunette took out a little bag of coke, they put it on my penis, then they took turns straddling me. While the blonde was on top, the brunette disappeared and came back with a syringe. They laughed. The blonde asked me if I was a member of the elite. I told her yes, I thought so, yes. They laughed again. The brunette drew some of her own blood, the blonde as well, so I followed their example. All of our blood was in the same syringe. The brunette heated something up over a Bunsen burner, I realized later it was heroin. She cooked it up, and then with a mischievous look, told me that from now on, I'd be a member of the elite. The extreme elite. They both laughed. The blonde came and sat down in front of me, her legs open. "Come on, it's your initiation to the elite," she said. When I leaned over and tasted her, the brunette slapped me on the ass and injected me. It was overwhelming; it was such a rush. The blonde held my head tight between her thighs while the brunette got out a razor blade and started to cut me up. Hundreds of incisions, everywhere. Blood flowed with every cut, and then they started sucking on them. And then, nothing. I don't remember a thing. I woke up at my own place, covered in scabs. I don't know how I got there. I was sore everywhere from the cuts, I went to the clinic. When I told the doctor what had happened, he looked at me like I'd just told him I'd shot myself in the head. (*Holding back tears.*) The extreme elite! It seems they mix up heroin with HIV-infected blood. (*Crying.*) HIV-infected blood! Fuck! (*Still crying, but angry.*) What they hell did those cunts do that for! Fucking junkies! Ludwig! (*A beat.*) Please, I really want to talk to you …

He hangs up. The answering machine beeps. Silence.

LUDWIG
(*calm*) Cow?

COW
(*gently*) Yes, Ludwig?

LUDWIG

(*reserved*) I'd like to hear my father's voice.

COW

(*oh so understanding*) Of course. Would you like him to tell you a story?

LUDWIG

(*almost nostalgic*) Yes, a story … The story he never told me.

COW

(*Playing the father as happy story-teller.*) "Ludwig? Hey kiddo. Come here and I'll tell you a story. Has anyone ever told you how we came to be a family of healers? Oh, you didn't know? You don't believe we have a healing gift? Oh yes! It's as true as true can be, let me tell you that the Tessiers are healers because your great-grandfather could work miracles. Oh yes! You don't believe me? Well, you know, when all the other great-grandfathers were telling their kids about the lives of the saints, your great-grandfather told stories about his miracles. He must've performed a dozen miracles a day! Loaves and fishes and bringing folks back to life. You think you know miracles? You name it, he did it! Because your great-grandfather, not many people know this, but his name was Jesus H. Christ!"

> *The* MUSE *has gone to get a machete that she sharpens on the grindstone. Two handcuffs descend from the ceiling. The* COW *is manacled to them. Voodoo music. The* COW *goes on as though all is normal.*

COW

"Oh, yes, he was Jesus Christ! The one, the only, the real deal. Except that it was a bit weird to be named that, so your great-grandfather changed his name to Hosanna

Tessier. But you know, everyone was jealous of Hosanna
Tessier or Jesus Christ, if you will. Everyone thought he
was pretty damn lucky to be able to perform miracles
like that, and chat merrily away with God, so everyone
started talking shit about him. It was quite a situation!"

*The MUSE gives the machete to LUDWIG. He hacks at the
COW's teats which spurt milk and blood. The COW does
not suffer, she continues her story.*

COW
"Hosanna Tessier's cousins—Marc and Luc Tremblay,
Mathieu Ducasse and Jean Tessier—started taking notes:
they figured they would write it all up in a best-seller.
Then one day, Jean realized that all the cousins were
doing the same thing and got depressed, so he went out
and got shitfaced, he went on a real bender, taking notes
all the while. Yessiree, Jean never left home without his
notepad. Except that the notes that he was taking that
night, what with the beer, the drugs, the women, he
called them *The Book of Revelations*. Well, it is what it is."

*The music, now frenzied, draws LUDWIG into that state;
the COW is reduced to a bloody and skeletal cadaver. The
phone rings again. The music stops.*

MAE'S VOICE
Ludwig, darling Ludwig, I went to Chartres, to Chartres
my darling, to the cornerstone of Chartres. The
cornerstone right under the stained glass window
depicting the life of St. Apollinaire. Through the hole at
the top I could see the light of heaven descending. It was
summer solstice and a ray of sunlight shone down
through the window and landed at my feet. God—not
your little god, the old-man-with-the-white-beard-and-
cane, not him, but Wisdom, the Higher Power … Oh, I

don't even know … Anyway, Ludwig, the sun took one of its rays and laid it gently at my feet, it caressed my toes. Chartres, Ludwig. Chartres Cathedral. I was floating. I'm still floating. The sacred geometrical harmonies … you'd be stunned. The architecture … it's like paradise's antechamber. One to six and one to eight with columns all around me: it seemed like I could touch the divine. The arches, Ludwig. And the labyrinth on the floor, carved right into the floor of the church. Sometimes we find places that seem familiar, like we've already been there. Before. Before memory. Before our reincarnation. Ludwig, I knew that labyrinth, that spiral. As a young woman, a virgin. Before memories. As a young virgin, I drew that labyrinth. I drew it with a branch in the sand. Because before churches, before marble, before all of that, there was sand. The guide laughed at me. He said that the cathedral has been there for over fifteen hundred years. I know that I drew it, the circle, the labyrinth: it's my circle, I know it. Ludwig, I've found my centre. (*Pause.*) Good-bye Ludwig. It's over. I loved you, you know. You do know. I'm doing well here, I'm okay, don't worry.

> *A long silence. Neither the* MUSE *nor the* POPE *dare go to* LUDWIG.

LUDWIG
She's doing well.

MUSE
(*worried*) Yes, she seems to be doing very well.

POPE
(*tense*) She's found herself, Ludwig.

MUSE
(*gentle but perplexed*) It's over.

LUDWIG
(*serene*) Already?

A beat. No one dares move or speak.

LUDWIG
(*very softly*) I'm not ready.

MUSE
(*gently*) What did you say?

The POPE starts sharpening the razor again. A choir of uncannily nubile ANGELS comes onto the forestage. They are three nubile ANGELS, each with a pistol in her hand. They are light, fresh. They giggle.

MUSE
Where did you come from?

UNCANNILY NUBILE ANGEL CHOIR
We are the angels, the angels of despair,
Nubile are we, we angels of death,
We burn inside, we're filled with flames
We hold the keys to the Gates of Hell,
We have no mercy, no pity, no heart
We are the angels of despair,
We are the nubile angels of death.
Cha-cha-cha!

LUDWIG
(*filled with desire, throws himself at one of the nubile sopranos*) One last time, before I die …

MUSE
Please, Ludwig. This is not the time.

LUDWIG chases frantically after the ANGELS. A nude Benny Hill, his body shaven, running after three little girls with guns in their hands.

LUDWIG
Call your mom, tell her you're spending the night at a friend's house.

LUDWIG catches an ANGEL by the waist, the ANGEL struggles.

MUSE
(*authoritarian*) Ludwig, that's enough!

LUDWIG
I'll take them all!

POPE
A little solemnity, Ludwig, if you please.

MUSE
And more to the point, a bit of dignity.

LUDWIG stops, lets go of the ANGEL, stands in front of a mirror; he contemplates his image. The POPE joins him with the killing tool, hands it to him.

POPE
Do you have anything to confess before ending your life?

LUDWIG
You're going to be my confessor?

POPE
Beggars can't be choosers.

LUDWIG
What a fucked up suicide.

POPE

What more do you want? You have your Pope, your
personal Muse, your scrawny Cow, your uncannily nubile
angel choir …

LUDWIG

We need more cows.

COW

(*briefly resuscitated, despite being mangled*) That's exactly
what I was thinking!

POPE

Shh! You're dead!

MUSE

(*suspicious*) Why cows, Ludwig?

LUDWIG

Because that one is dead.

POPE

Do you realize, Ludwig, every cow you ever got, you cut
it to bits. That was your last one. If you can't take proper
care of your cows, you can't have any more!

LUDWIG

I want cows! I want cows!! I want cows!!!

POPE

Too late. You'll have to make do with your Pope and
your Muse. Now let's get down to business. I'm listening,
my son.

LUDWIG

(*in terror*) I haven't accomplished anything! I haven't
achieved anything!!

He smashes the mirror in front of him. The POPE backs away. The nubile ANGELS move towards LUDWIG, rub up against him, cut him with the razor that they swiped from the POPE. LUDWIG, frantic, rants.

LUDWIG
(*quoting Leonard Cohen without knowing it*) "I stepped on a beetle."

LUDWIG AND THE UNCANNILY NUBILE ANGEL CHOIR
"Pray for me."

LUDWIG
"I polluted the spring with my urine."

LUDWIG AND THE UNCANNILY NUBILE ANGEL CHOIR
"Pray for me."

The ANGELS continue to mutilate LUDWIG's body.

LUDWIG
"I felt up my sister."

LUDWIG AND THE UNCANNILY NUBILE ANGEL CHOIR
"Pray for me."

LUDWIG
"I dreamt of becoming a WASP."

LUDWIG AND THE UNCANNILY NUBILE ANGEL CHOIR
"Pray for me."

LUDWIG
"I didn't help a dying squirrel."

LUDWIG AND THE UNCANNILY NUBILE ANGEL CHOIR
"Pray for me."

LUDWIG
"I'd gladly eat strips of human flesh."

LUDWIG AND THE UNCANNILY NUBILE ANGEL CHOIR
"Pray for me."

LUDWIG
"I squeezed the yellow out of a worm."

LUDWIG AND THE UNCANNILY NUBILE ANGEL CHOIR
"Pray for me."

LUDWIG
"I gave my grandmother's rosary to the Anglos."

LUDWIG AND THE UNCANNILY NUBILE ANGEL CHOIR
"Pray for me."

LUDWIG
"I inherited dirty money."

LUDWIG AND THE UNCANNILY NUBILE ANGEL CHOIR
"Pray for me."

LUDWIG
"I smoke shit."

LUDWIG AND THE UNCANNILY NUBILE ANGEL CHOIR
"Pray for me."

LUDWIG
"I forced my brother to watch."

LUDWIG AND THE UNCANNILY NUBILE ANGEL CHOIR
"Pray for me."

LUDWIG
"I masturbated to *Paradise Lost*."

A rope has descended in front of the POPE. *He's been looking at it for a while already. He gets ready to hang himself from it, but the nubile* ANGELS *notice and immediately shoot him down. He dies from the three bullets.*

LUDWIG AND THE UNCANNILY NUBILE ANGEL CHOIR
"Pray for me."

LUDWIG
"I don't recycle my newspapers."

LUDWIG AND THE UNCANNILY NUBILE ANGEL CHOIR
"Pray for me."

LUDWIG
"I added a notch to my belt each time I fucked without a condom."

LUDWIG AND THE UNCANNILY NUBILE ANGEL CHOIR
"Pray for me."

LUDWIG
"I don't believe in anything."

LUDWIG AND THE UNCANNILY NUBILE ANGEL CHOIR
"Pray for me."

LUDWIG
"I don't believe in anything."

LUDWIG AND THE UNCANNILY NUBILE ANGEL CHOIR
"Pray for me."

LUDWIG
"There's nothing left."

UNCANNILY NUBILE ANGEL CHOIR
"There's nothing left."

POPE
(*returning from the other side*) "There's nothing left."

Another bullet from each nubile ANGEL.

MUSE
(*takes the stage, walks forward*) The thirst for life drives one to excess.

UNCANNILY NUBILE ANGEL CHOIR
A woman walks back and forth, displaying herself.

MUSE
A woman walks back and forth, displaying herself.

UNCANNILY NUBILE ANGEL CHOIR
She wears leather. The leather is suffocating her. She knits. Her knitting suffocates her. A former Chinese delivery guy, now a door-to-door pharmacist, comes by with some pills ...

ALAIN LALONDE has in fact appeared onstage with a pill in his outstretched hand.

CHINESE DELIVERY GUY
There are no small parts, only small actors.

MUSE
(*calmly*) Fuck you, Alain Lalonde.

UNCANNILY NUBILE ANGEL CHOIR
She takes the pills. The pills poison her. She finds herself dying. Fuck you, Alain Lalonde. Fuck you, Alain Lalonde.

The DELIVERY GUY disappears forever. The MUSE dies.

UNCANNILY NUBILE ANGEL CHOIR
(*taking out their guns*) Oh! Her hand, her hand, her hand!
Look at her hand!

> *The MUSE's hand spasms like the hand of one who has*
> *just died a cruel death. The ANGELS shoot mercilessly.*
> *The hand drops.*

LUDWIG
(*exhausted*) Can't even die in peace, huh, Muse?

UNCANNILY NUBILE ANGEL CHOIR
Her hand, her hand, her lovely dead hand, her lovely
dead hand.

> *The ANGELS snigger. They go to kiss LUDWIG, then exit,*
> *as frivolous as when they first arrived.*

LUDWIG
(*Alone in the spotlight. He is still naked, the razor in his*
hand.) Can't even die in peace! I want to be free to die.
Free. I want to break with Fate! I'm taking charge of my
own destiny. I am God. Breaking away, deconstructing,
understanding, deconstructing, undoing, understanding,
deconstructing, freeing myself from mortgages, debts,
religions, party lines—the Blues the Reds—the others,
Europeans, Americans, Canadians, Québécois, wackos,
realists, theorists, architects, poets, discerning fans of
irony, sarcasm, versimilitude, the true, the pure, the false,
the theatrical, deconstructing, undoing, laying bare,
exposing conventions: Rope! Macbeth! Beelzebub, come
quickly, I am yours! Virginia Woolf three times in the
mirror! Ouija! RRSP rat race! I was considered useful to
society, I became the engineer of the tower of Pisa,
Montreal's Olympic Stadium, the *Exxon Valdez*, Lada
cars, the Quebec City Bridge, the Quebec Bridge twice,
the Quebec City Bridge a third time! I want to lick the

Virgin's cunt, Joseph's asshole, the Dalai Lama's toes, Saddam's moustache, the president's gonorrhea, Mohammed's whores, the Queen Mother's ear! All politicians dream of becoming Hitler, Stalin, Franco, or Reagan. All football players and soldiers have a collection of male blow-up dolls. The spiritual father of Kay-bec was an intolerant fascist xenophobe, the spiritual father of Canada was a drunk. Taking it up the ass is just fine, as long as you don't make me moo. We are all corpses! Warm corpses! Our girlfriends and boyfriends are necrophiles. Our parents too. Families are havens of abuse. I lost my Saint Anthony medal, I replaced it with the party card. I sell out the party left, right, and centre. Shit on all the flags, even the black flag, shit on all the lawns, on the family photos, on endorsed cheques. Spit in the face of all the Masters. Break away. Kill before being killed, kill myself, kill myself often. Die. Die. (*Goes to the bathtub, gets in.*) I have to die. Die often. Never get rigor mortis. Get used to death. Taste death. Inject myself with life. Inoculate myself to it. Die. Make a symbol of myself. Kill the symbol. Justify. Make myself useful. Cling. Cling to life. No! There's no way. No way to live. No way to give. No way. I feel life germinating. I have to kill it! Kill the seed of rebellion. Kill the muse, kill inspiration. Silence my conscience. Tear my childhood to shreds. Burn my memories. Mythologize myself. Break down death. My death will be called Joseph Honour Narcissus Tessier. Kill myself. Do justice to myself. Believe in death: the redemption of the reign of shit. Kill myself, come back as a guilty conscience. Take revenge. Kill myself. Make my death useful. Kill indifference. Kill indifference. (*He slices the artery in his left wrist.*) Kill indifference! (*Then the other wrist ... blood gushes into the bathtub.*)

The phone rings. The answering machine picks up.

FATHER'S VOICE

Hello? Ludwig? You're still not there. Well, it's your father again. Listen, I didn't want to scare you the other day with my message. You must have heard it by now ... I'm dying, my son. Do you realize that? Okay, I've said it, I'm dying. Wanna hear a good one? I've never cared so much about living! Living! Not to live like a maniac, not living just to die slowly. I want to learn to live again! Learn how to talk to you again, to listen to you, you and your mother. Learn how to tell you I love you. I think we're ready now ... Ludwig, pick up.

Silence.

VOICES OF COW AND POPE

Pick up ...

MUSE'S VOICE

... Ludwig ...

VOICES OF COW AND POPE

... pick up!

LUDWIG picks up the receiver.

FATHER'S VOICE

Ludwig?

Silence.

FATHER'S VOICE

Talk to me, Ludwig.

LUDWIG

(*feebly*) Daddy.

FATHER'S VOICE
   (*filled with terror*) What's wrong?!

LUDWIG
   (*dying*) I'd like to learn to live again too.

   *The sky turns a dazzling red. The scenery and props
   return to wherever they came from. We hear a sad and
   glorious requiem being sung. LUDWIG doesn't move, he
   looks like Marat as painted by David: the friend of the
   people dying in his bathtub. Blackout.*

RESURRECTION

(Ressusciter)

The premiere production of *Ressusciter* by Théâtre la Catapulte opened on March 19, 1996 at the Café Deluxe in Ottawa. It was directed by Anne-Marie White with Chantal Aubut in the role of Mae.

This shorter version of the original play was presented as a staged reading on May 24, 1997 at the Théâtre du Nouvel Ontario in Sudbury. It was directed by the author with Marie-Christine Lê-Huu in the role of Mae.

An earlier version of this translation, *Resurrection,* was read by the author on May 12, 2008 at Playwrights' Workshop Montreal as part of a Playwrights Guild of Canada reading series.

Note:

This monologue contains direct quotes and paraphrases from *Embedded* and *Apocalypse* by the same author, as well as from poems by Hildegard von Bingen; from the books of Paul, Matthew, and Ruth; and from Tolstoy's *Resurrection*.

While we were speaking, the image of him in his youth has come back to me ... I saw him—I see him now before me—see him as he was at the age of twenty ... I must have loved that man—once! (...) And—hated him!—May peace be with him!

—August Strindberg
The Dance of Death

For this corruptible must put on incorruption, and this mortal must put on immortality.

—Paul,
First Letter to the
Corinthians (15:33)

I

MAE

His father's the one who told me—on our anniversary.
Ludwig's father, the same man who, the previous
Tuesday, proclaimed his belief in a happy future; the
same man who, the Tuesday prior to that, had left several
messages on his son's answering machine describing the
stupidest antics imaginable and confessing to the
unspeakable—after first asking his son to love him
unconditionally even though he had never taught him a
thing about unconditional love (in fact, both father and
son refuse to believe that love exists; in their view, only
desire matters: desire for affection, desire to give
affection, sexual desire, desire for intimacy, solitary
desires, desire, desire, nothing but fucking desire).
Ludwig's father, the same man who let his body and soul
be mutilated last winter by two junkies who resented
their fathers just like Ludwig resented his—Ludwig's
father, who kept on repeating *two junkies, two junkies*—
but let's get to Ludwig himself.

Ludwig had never really thought about his father
dying. All he knew was that it would happen someday
when he least expected it. He'd never thought that his
father, mutilated by his own desire, could become a
pincushion for two harpies that he'd spent the night
with. Hundreds of lacerations all over his body wrought

by two razor blades. Ludwig never imagined that this man who had never once acted as a father might be content to die such a shameful death. He knew now that it was too late, that all he could do was feel regret and carve his father's last words into his headstone.

One thing you can say about Ludwig: derisive and cynical as he was, he had a highly developed sense of tragedy.

The night of our fourth anniversary that never was because we'd broken up three weeks earlier—it would have been the fourth anniversary of our first meeting—that night, the phone rang. A simple phone call, transmitting a voice: his father's guilty voice, the voice of someone who's just realized he's an adult. A voice full of responsibility and authority and compassion. A voice, just a voice. But I knew there would be no more leering, no more sour breath on my neck, no more roving hands groping for my own nervous and evasive ones. (He had a bad habit of coming on to his son's girlfriends.) Ludwig's father was well hidden behind his new adult voice.

And if I hadn't been so despicable, if I had really gone where I'd said I was going, if I'd really been in Europe or Asia or somewhere, anywhere, trying to find myself and finally truly happy like I'd told him, I'd have merely come home to a message on the machine and I wouldn't have had the live confession of a guilty and impotent father. A message left by a father who grew up too late, telling me that his son, the only man I'd ever loved, is dead. Yes, I loved Ludwig; and yet there's this rage in my heart …

"Mae, pull yourself together, get up off the floor!" Easy to say. Yeah right, get up! Why don't you tell your son to get up. That's right, tell him! Like Jesus what's-his-face: Young man, I command thee, rise! No! There's nothing left for me to get up for. I'll lie here as long as your son's death weighs me down. I'll lie here for as long as everything is about death or suicide or oppression or the sorry lot of humanity or Ludwig's theories on life, love, religion, philosophy, "on the construction of implosive bridges, on the necessary deconstruction of institutions … "

To the father.

I'll lie here, 'cause I'm scared that Ludwig is watching me through the window laughing at me. I can hear him spitting out his threats, just like every time I was going to leave him: "I'll bleed myself like a cow. Like a cow, you hear me?!"

Yes, Ludwig, I heard. Like a cow.

I'm scared that he's there at the window with his brothers, Hugo and Stefan, even though I know he was an only child, but he still liked making up little stories about them. I'm scared that he'll come in through the window pretending he's Uncle Salin wanting to rape me. Ludwig! Get out of here! I can't live with you anymore, you're suffocating me! You're always talking about killing yourself, you're killing me slowly, dragging my life out of me. I can't do it any more, Ludwig, I can't blame myself for your death! I knew you were going to slit your wrists, but what was I supposed to do?

Ludwig's dead. His father called him again, one last time. He'd been leaving messages for three weeks, but Ludwig hadn't returned his calls. That wasn't so strange in itself, given that during our four years together, Ludwig had never once called his father back. He wanted to prove, as he had always suspected, that parents were like bottomless wells. Three weeks of messages from his father, who assured me that he wasn't just calling to chat. The last ones were cruel and biting, even if they weren't meant to be. His last call was meant to shake Ludwig out of his stupor, because his father intuitively understood Ludwig like I never did. He knew that Ludwig had heard his messages and that he was holed up in his apartment. He was sure that Ludwig needed help and affection and paternal love even though neither of them really knew what paternal love actually was … but it was twenty-five years too late for horsey-rides and bedtime stories. His father had suddenly grown up overnight and his last call to his lost son was his first call as an adult. "I think we're ready now … Ludwig, pick up." He was using his new adult voice, a responsible voice, full of authority and compassion. Until it broke—

"Pick up!" Sounding like a hysterical teenager. "Pick up!"

Then, Ludwig's weak voice, for once it was weak and had only one message to convey, a message with no ambiguity—I can hardly imagine Ludwig so vulnerable, but it seems he was just before he died—a simple sentence, his last words sounded repentant, a fallen optimist approaching his death. "Daddy," he had whispered, "I want to learn how to live again too." The father panics, speeds his Porsche over and finds the bloodbath …

Inside, three schoolgirl uniforms lying in the entrance; on the kitchen table, a black leather bustier and a long knit scarf in the hallway. Hanging from the ceiling, a cow carcass, cut into quarters, and right in the living room, seven lamps arranged in a perfect circle around an old bathtub, a lovely old tub filled with hot water, where Ludwig lay steeping in his own blood. Ludwig had romantic ideas, despite his aversion to sentimentality.

His body was shaved, the bloody blade fallen to the ground, the cordless phone at the bottom of the tub, and on a chair, his clean clothes ironed and folded. There was a will on his desk, a strange will but completely his style. The will of someone with nothing to give, nothing to lose. The will of an egotist who would have given anything so that no one would kill themselves ever again. I guess he had good intentions, but the truth is, no one gives a shit about his suicide. Because he couldn't build anything, he chose to destroy. Because he couldn't fit in, he wanted to carve us out a space where we'd feel his pain. In his will, Ludwig asked to be crucified in public, at the mall, in effigy to remind people of their complacency.

Whenever he told me his ridiculous ideas, I would laugh. Nervously. But I still laughed. It was better to laugh.

He'd left a note on the fridge, in a child's scrawl: "I am what survives of me." In the bathroom, twelve test tubes full of Ludwig's sperm. Twelve test tubes, that Ludwig had intended to spawn twelve little terrorists that would undo everything he hadn't had the chance to undo himself ... So? Isn't it the dream of every father to see his children take up his torch? Had he been a dentist, he'd have dreamed of a dentist son. But Ludwig wanted to give birth to terrorists.

Ludwig is dead, dead in his bath, naked and shaven. He'd been holed up in there for three weeks listening to phone messages, surrounded by all his little ceremonial props: What a spectacle!

To Ludwig.

That's what you'd have wanted us to say, right Ludwig? "The classic bloody bathtub scene!" "O Lamb of God who takes away the sins of the world!" Damn you, Ludwig! Did you get off on it? Did it make you feel like Jean-Paul Marat? He died in his bathtub too. The Friend of the People in all his splendour, his head in a turban, his body limp but proud, and his blood vermilion ... You haven't done anything new, Ludwig, I've seen the David painting. Was I supposed to be your Charlotte Corday?

Should I have knocked at the door three times before delivering you to your death ... I knew you'd been thinking about it for a long time, I knew it every time we had sex and you asked me to die with you ... You weren't religious but you would have liked to take away the sins of the world. You purified yourself, you shaved yourself, then you mutilated yourself. Why? To make yourself into a martyr? To save us all from the hands of the Philistines? Why did you kill yourself, Ludwig? Out of cowardice? Because you were no Samson, born to save the world? Since you didn't deserve your hair you had to shave it all off? Since you weren't destined for greatness, did you think life wasn't worth living?

You weren't cut out to be a hero, but I loved you, and that's something, isn't it? To be loved unconditionally? You fool.

To the audience.

And me? I'm the girlfriend, the infamous girlfriend who couldn't help him. I never could, ever. Something stopped me. Ludwig stopped me. He had his little sanctuary that he'd retreat to, and I couldn't get in. There were so many things to learn about him, and I'd have managed, over the years. But it's too late now. I've had enough of living in the middle of a suicidal maelstrom, I don't need any more of his horror stories. His stories almost did me in.

I'm going to have to figure out my own story. If I'm going to survive.

II

MAE

> For the moment, my story is embedded in someone else's story.
>
> I'm the dead guy's girlfriend, guilty! I'm the girl with her whole life ahead of her and who isn't doing anything interesting with it, guilty! I thought I could outsmart him but he outsmarted me—guilty! I too, lied to make my life into what I wanted it to be—guilty!
>
> Right now I don't want anything. I gave and gave till I had nothing left, until that fine, sunny morning when Ludwig left me. It was a Monday morning, after a weekend just like all the other weekends these past four years, a weekend of lovemaking and abject cruelty, a weekend of games that went on so long we forgot why we were playing in the first place, we forgot why we were so hungry, we forgot why we had no energy left to go on. That same Monday morning my cat, Victor, instinctively came back home to his old life. Ludwig had come between Victor and me, but that morning Victor returned to his rightful place. And then there was that other guy, the Chinese delivery guy. He was "in love with me," or so it seemed, but I didn't have what it took to be loved, I didn't have the courage, I was empty and yet my breasts were swelling. So I invented this new story but it was too late to invent happiness. My usual story was starting to unnerve me.
>
> Ludwig never believed the story. It was beautiful, but it scared him. I would tell him I was pregnant with his child. I told it to him many times so he'd believe me, as often as he'd let me. I must have told it at least a dozen

times over the four years. And each time I told him, his reaction was the same, as if it was his favourite bedtime story and he could see all the plot twists coming. He knew all the twists and turns and when he got bored with them he'd invent even better ones. I'd also tell him that I loved him in spite of himself, that I'd always be there for him, that no other woman could ever love him as much as I did. I always tried to stay one step ahead of him, because with Ludwig, nothing was ever stable. I couldn't trust him to be satisfied with stability.

I went to the apartment to exorcise what was eating at me. I listened to the final messages on his answering machine, I know he'd heard them. I paid special attention to the messages I'd left from the airport, from New York, Paris, Brittany, the Chartres Cathedral. I had wanted to invent some happiness for myself. I definitely didn't want him to be worried about me. I wanted to be happily travelling around like that, but I couldn't because of the baby. This time I was sure I was pregnant for real. I was going on a liberating journey for all three of us: Ludwig, the baby, and me. I made up a lovely little story for us, the trip to Europe where Mae finds herself, enjoys herself, is led back to her source. I couldn't come back unchanged because I was giving us *permission* to change for the better! Out with our old ways, the co-dependent relationship, with death always lurking in one corner of the bedroom. After Chartres, there was to be no contact for a month, a full month of distance and desire, of adventuring across a continent. And then I'd have asked him to come and meet me in France, telling him then that he was going to be a father. But none of it was true, not even the pregnancy. It was a scare, what they call a hysterical pregnancy. A ball of nerves and emptiness all swollen up inside me, making me think that I was pregnant … But no. The only thing that Ludwig had

engendered was a gaping void. Nothingness. Even
though I was convinced there was a baby there, just like
I'd actually started to believe I was on this amazing
European voyage. It was all so twisted! Ludwig is dead. I
was just a few blocks away, holed up in my apartment,
reading about Europe, surfing the net, stealing little bits
of other people's trips. I never set foot in the airport,
never mind New York, Paris, Brittany, or Chartres.

Christ! If I had only gone to see him, Ludwig wouldn't
be dead. I was too convincing. He believed me. For the
first time ever, he believed me. I'm not going to play
anymore, no more pretending. I hate myself for being so
convincing. Ludwig would have laughed. Tragic stories
of death always cracked him up. But what made him
happiest was when the hero outwitted death.

In his last message, he really did sound vulnerable: his
voice was tiny and simple. "I want to learn to live again
too."

That doesn't sound like the last words of someone
about to commit suicide.

I also lost our non-existent child.

Only my memories are left.

To Ludwig.

My memories of you, Ludwig. The memory of those hot
July nights when you were sleeping, your body shutting
down, your limbs slowly relaxing one by one, your brow
furrowing one last time and then silence, your breathing
free of all malice. Free of everything cruel in you; all your
cruelty was erased by the night. Your smile, when it
slipped out when you couldn't hold it in any longer …
The memory of our political discussions, our discussions
of the politics of love, our aversion to lies, our ludicrous
declarations: "The diplomats of affection are hysterical!"
we shouted, standing on the bed stark naked, and we

were probably ridiculously nostalgic, like all couples who always need things to be intense, who believe their relationship must avoid monotony at all costs. Even if it means living in a state of perpetual crisis. Living intensely. 'Cause that's what living is!

To the audience.

All that's left is the mythology we built together over those four years. The first night, the morning after, the cat's exile, the ex-girlfriend with the brown eyes, Ludwig's imaginary brothers, Hugo and Stefan, Uncle Salin, the neighbour Dumont: the mean and hungry wolves of his youth, then the Chinese delivery guy, the cat's return, Ludwig's final departure …

Well, that sums up our relationship and I don't even have a leading role!

I don't remember who I was anymore, who I'd been before meeting Ludwig.

I think I wanted kids, that I wanted to act till I dropped, till I was too old, and even then, even then I wanted to be rolled onstage in a wheelchair if need be. I was … pretty much like I am now, but with less of an aftertaste. Who was I? I seem to remember having kept a diary over three years, I'll read it tonight. I can't remember my teenage years. Ludwig is dead. I'll read it tonight …

III

MAE

Last night I read my diary …

I was so sweet with my fairy-tale ideas, my little-girl dreams: fantasies of horses galloping through fields dotted with buttercups and handsome men, my little "horsies" that adored me; brown because I knew that only brown horses were trustworthy and faithful.

I was so sweet with my dreams of being an actress, from the time I was eight, nine, then seventeen, nineteen … I was so beautiful! Not in the least jaded, I didn't even know that a person could be jaded. I was free and naïve and more than anything else in the world I wanted to be on stage so people could see how good and beautiful and articulate I was. Burn up the stage! A storm of applause that felt like a warm rain, a thousand tingles of approval. Clapclapclapclap and clap and clap. "Thank you! I love you too!" I only wanted the nice roles, the nice characters, strong but romantic women, happy strong-willed women who feel entitled to their dreams and make demands, heroines that never have to go through hard times, heroines who people respect and don't push around, heroines who don't suffer but occasionally have moments of melancholy … I wanted to be a surface actress: I didn't even know that there was anything under the surface! I was pure. Not a drop of despair—apart from a couple of episodes of prepubescent angst that I mistook to be despair—nothing but joy and unbearable lightness. Nothing of this dirty, filth-ridden, hypocritical, base world that Ludwig made me see. He rubbed my face in it: "Look how ugly it is! Admit that it's ugly! Admit it! It's rotten to the core! Death runs in your veins too. Death!"

But I still believe that underneath his cynical shell, Ludwig was an optimist, demanding the most from life, from himself, and from others.

He'd have liked to wake up the whole world—He'd have liked to remind the adults that if they'd hoped to change the world for the better, they'd failed. He'd have liked to tell them they were beautiful while they were building a dream but today they're ugly and pathetic with their RRSPs, and their Saabs (*sounding more and more like Ludwig*), with their neocon government that's back up on top after hibernating for thirty-five years, their neocon government that's prepared to declare a recession merely to justify cleaning up anything that doesn't suit their plans, their tyrannical government pumped up with the morality and ideas of nouveau riche dimwits, their puppet regime; NO, we did NOT choose to become American!

To Ludwig.

Ah Ludwig, you would get carried away, you could say the strangest things, you would mix up the grotesque and the sublime without even realizing it, you'd insult anyone who didn't agree with you, you'd rail against those adults who were nostalgic for those years when *change was brewing* but who aren't brewing anything today except maybe a vat of home-made beer, who've stopped believing in lefty cooperative endeavours because communes don't have pension plans, these adults who are happy with their fate because they monopolize both authority and subversion. Oh, I've heard that one a few times! You really got going sometimes, Ludwig, but you forgot that we're responsible too, that we shouldn't get sucked into playing those adult games.

To the audience.

I'm not ashamed to say I don't remember Expo 67, or the first moonwalk: I wasn't born yet. I learned about the October Crisis in history class. My parents' memories aren't mine.

These ancient things are no more, all I can do now is embrace the future. Take the new in my arms and hold it tight, caress it gently. Give myself to anything with the prefix neo-, let myself be taken, penetrated. I'm letting go, Ludwig, I'm giving myself to the future because you never had the courage to do that, you could never renew yourself. Die, yes, you could die, but not kill, you could never kill. It's not the same thing, Ludwig.

I won't become the long-suffering widow, the premature widow drowning in her misery: I'm not even an adult yet! Let me become an adult before asking me to rot from the inside out. I don't want to be deprived of history and happiness, I don't want to dream of what might have been. I don't want to be anyone's widow.

The night will be my home, it will be my house of rest. The night will tend to my wounds. I'll gather my strength, the scars run deep, they are smooth and tender.

One day, I'll have the strength to leave the house. Someone will want me, someone will need me. Someone will call out my name, tell me I'm beautiful, that he melts under my gaze, that he loves me and needs to be loved by me, only me. I know that I'm impossibly naïve, but I don't care.

Most likely I'll meet someone else, who will look just like him, I'll worship him, I'll give, I'll give unconditionally, I'll end up with someone else who doesn't know how to love or give. Tomorrow morning, I'll write, to forget that I have no story. I'll write because sometimes when I

close my eyes, I can see. I can see … I can see …
dammit, no I can't.

I'll write furiously. For a long time. Not in snippets, I'll
make the fury last … I'll start by redoing what was
undone, I'll write to wake up people's consciences. If I
am going to write what I have to write, I can't hide the
blemishes, I'll write the truth—or I won't write at all.
The truth, everything will be true, or at least almost true,
or at least sincere.

I'll go as deep as possible within me. First, the
character. I'll wear black crinoline. No. She'll wear black
crinoline, the dead guy's widow, walking with her head
high because she always walks like that, with an open
gaze and a wide smile. Proud, meticulous, generous … I
recognize that girl! I knew her once. Years ago, she
commanded the stage like a diva, with the precision of a
Swiss clockmaker! She was luminous. I remember her
honeyed voice, her musical words, the flow of her move-
ments, her huge deep eyes that gently took in everything.
Hello! Mae! It's me, I'm over here!

She's looking at me! Oh god, those eyes! The terrible
blackness of her eyes … they are deep, infinitely deep
and dangerous. "No, Mae, I'm not ready, not yet!" Her
eyes! They're a black hole. I don't want to. Take her away,
I don't know her! It's not Mae.

I don't believe you, it's lies, only lies. I'm beautiful, you
don't know me.

Get away, you witch! Get out! Leave Ludwig alone!
What are you doing? Don't you see that Ludwig is
dying? You have no right! Leave him alone, can't you see
he's bleeding? No! Leave him in his bath, leave him
alone.

Oh! She's kissing him!

He wakes up: Ludwig, I loved you … His gaze, like
that of the false Mae, empty, hollow … I love you more

today, Ludwig, I'm happy, I'm free. They're laughing
together, Ludwig and the false Mae. With crazed eyes.
They're mad. Do I also have the right to dip into
madness? Ludwig! Did you like my lies? How about my
trip to Europe? My lies were the best! You believed me?!
I'm suffering too, I have suffered, I will suffer, amen,
Hallelujah, as it was in the beginning and forever and
ever … Ludwig! Jesus Christ! I was so soft, so precious,
so innocent. Okay, more or less innocent. What did you
do to me? And you, you witch, go back to where you
came from! No, I don't recognize you. Get out of here
with your crocodile tears. No, no, no! Your name isn't
Mae, no! I'll rip your head off! Leave us alone, Ludwig,
I'll get rid of her for you. I'll set out a rat trap with a nice
big piece of cheese. Cheese with holes. Ha ha ha, she'll
get her foot caught in a cheese hole and then SNAP! And
that'll be the end. Out, you imposter! Do I have to kick
you out? I don't recognize me, hold up your mirror,
witch! I don't even look like myself in your mirror! The
eyes. My eyes. My face! The fever, the spasms, the cries,
the devil in my body! No more speeches, Ludwig, that's
over. I create, I cry, I write, I cry that this doesn't make
any sense and I have nothing to say except that you said
in your moments of grace that I had exquisite fuzz, that I
was a sweet peach, and here I am, just the same as that
false Mae prancing around in her wet dress: "I am dead
too, the river flows over me, the river flows," splash
splash, poor Ophelia, splash. I've already said my piece
but Ludwig didn't believe my story, it was a lovely story:
I create and I procreate. I was gestating something to
reconcile us, I was bearing the fruit of our love, but the
fruit fermented, look, it turned to peach vinegar. Splash,
under the river, my bridal veil, my wedding bed, splash,
under the river, the rapids, the falls, the ocean, I feel a

geyser rising, a volcano, wave after violent wave of lava, and it's rising in me, rising, rising rising.

Rising in me, like a dam breaking, like a volcano, wave after wave of lava rising and rising, and it erupts, erupts, up and up and up: and I see!

Finally I can see what had to emerge, my true self revealed, a tangible dream, real and fluid. If only I could open myself completely, drop my defenses. My prudishness, my fear of ridicule, my fear of myself. I see, I hear, the roar of the self surges through me.

"I will write simply, within the limits of my language. The roar does not come as the articulate cry of the poet, nor as the tirade of the orator, but rather as a flickering flame, or a porous cloud hanging in a July-blue sky."

A beat.

Beneath the blue sky, beneath the porous cloud, beneath the flickering flame where my desire burns, enveloped in the roar of the self, the cry in which we can hear ourselves without having to repeat, I glimpse myself: Mae. Standing in the middle of a field in July, with open hands, and fingers spread, I catch all of the falling stardust. I am ready. Mae! Oh, Mae. I'm coming! She runs to me without knowing it's me calling her, she knows that someone's calling and that it's important. And then she takes flight, she glides towards me. I glide towards me. I am her.

—Mae, do you recognize me?

—Yes, I know you, you're Mae, aren't you?

—Yes!

—Tell me something about myself ...

—When you were a little girl you loved horses but you called them "horsies" because you thought it was prettier.

—I still do!

—You wrote "horsies" in your diary and you drew them with huge penises without really knowing what they were.

—Shh! No one knows that!

—I missed you, Mae.

—Will you hold me in your arms?

We've found each other. This is really good.

—Hold me. You're so warm, give me some of your energy, I need it, I'm writing, you know?

To the audience.

She knew. She knew me, felt me, was even more like me than I am myself. I thought I would lose whatever remained of my balance. She held me in her arms and caressed me. I stopped doubting. The only thing left was to summon the July blue sky. The only thing left was to remember. Close your eyes, I'll find you there …

Author's Afterword

The initial scenes of this trilogy were written in 1991—a lifetime ago. I was nineteen and had vowed never to take a day job that didn't have a direct link with theatre or literature. I never have. This, of course, set up a moral and, more importantly, an economic obligation to write and stage my own plays and to accept any commission I received. The commissions with their constraints and deadlines turned out to be the best of schools. I left theatre school as soon as I felt too comfortable there. I officially dropped out a few hours before the opening night of my directing project in February 1992, a bacchanalian exploration involving nine actors and three musicians. This theatrical act, combined with my visual transformation from a mild-mannered long-haired and bearded Jesus look-alike to a skin-headed manifesto-writing ambitious and angry young man signalled my emergence as an "enfant terrible" within my small theatre community. *Embedded* (originally produced in 1994), *Apocalypse* (1995), and *Resurrection* (1996, a new version in 1997) were written in this mindset, as a necessary break from the commissioned, circumscribed work I was doing to make a living, but also as a reaction to a straight-laced artistic community, and as a way to probe a matrix of theatrical possibilities. These plays were my own little strange and sometimes troubling sandbox. Nothing was taboo. Nothing was censored. Those who came to play with me were expected to leave behind their preconceptions and be ready to try anything.

The writing and subsequent staging of these three particular plays took place between 1991 and 1997, an extraordinarily active and exciting creative period for me. Out of necessity and hyperactivity I wrote many plays, agit-prop "interventions" and radio plays. I also founded and managed Ottawa's Théâtre la Catapulte, a company devoted to experimentation and to the then up-and-coming generation of theatre practitioners. In 1998, I left the company—which had become government-funded and firmly established in a shared theatre space—burnt out and no longer able to reconcile my anti-establishment stance from within the very heart of the establishment. While I wrote and directed other plays during the same period, I feel that *Embedded*, *Apocalypse*, and *Resurrection* constitute the essence of what I sought to accomplish dramaturgically during my twenties. I was a young, arrogant, impatient punk who desperately wanted to establish an exciting dialogue with his community. The community showed little interest, so I lashed out ever more violently, hoping to provoke some semblance of life and debate in what I felt were complacent, indifferent, moribund theatrical and social establishments. I tried to do this with art and, I hoped, a certain panache.

Around the time *Apocalypse* (*Rappel*) was originally produced in Ottawa, Sarah Kane's *Blasted* was shaking up the dramaturgical and moral foundations of British drama at London's Royal Court Theatre and Dominic Champagne's cathartic *Cabaret neiges noires* was touring Québec and giving voice to a disenfranchised generation. I would only later discover Kane's work, but looking back on that period I realize to what extent the mid-nineties were ripe for outright attacks on what had become the hyper-professionalized theatre institution. Paradoxically, *Apocalypse* (*Rappel*) premiered at the National Arts Centre of Canada's Studio; it was the opening show in a festival of regional plays attended by artistic directors and theatre-folk. *Embedded* (*La Litière*) had been produced in the very university theatre department I had rejected and railed against in the media. However, I would later produce *Resur-rection* (*Ressusciter*) in the most marginal space I could find, the basement of a restaurant in Ottawa's By-Ward Market. This space had previously been an industrial techno hipster club which I associated with Ludwig and Mae's initial meeting. Staging the third play of the trilogy in such a space on a shoe-string budget after having "done" the National Arts Centre was a provocation in itself. *Ressusciter* corresponded to a new creative period in which I collaborated extensively with director Anne-Marie White on works which were stylistically multi-layered (*Le rêve totalitaire de dieu l'amibe*, 1995 and 1996, and *Tom Pouce, version fin de siècle*, 1997 and 1998).

With each new play, I wanted to reinvent myself. My objective was to have a recognizable signature but not a stifling "style." While there are a number of intertexual citations and evocations, I wanted each of these productions to be a self-contained aesthetic experience. Because of this, *Embedded*, *Apocalypse*, and *Resurrection* are very much separate plays, even though their characters and story link them together. The trilogy has an *über*-play, a prologue of sorts; *Dialogue, or a Treatise on Sadomasochistic Flirting* (1992), which was included in the original French language publication and which later spawned another series of plays, *Dialogues fantasques pour causeurs éperdus* (*Fantastical Dialogues for Smitten Conversation-alists*, 2008). As well, I wrote a manner of epilogue for Alain Lalonde, the Chinese Delivery Guy, "Alain Lalonde, barbier," as part of an evening of "Urban Tales" (*Contes d'appartenance*, 1999). However, the core of Ludwig and Mae's tale is to be found in this published trilogy.

I am now a middle-class, RRSP-contributing, suburb-dwelling university professor. Do I cringe when rereading certain passages of these plays? I feel that Ludwig's unfiltered vociferations, the Chinese Delivery Guy's anti-institutional stance, and the awkward and unreasonable stage directions were right for the plays in the context of their time and their productions. To tinker with these would be to open up a Pandora's box of endless revisions, so I have chosen to continue writing new plays rather than to revisit and adapt earlier ones.

I resisted translating my earlier plays myself to avoid the very strong temptation to rewrite them. Shelley Tepperman and Ellen Warkentin have done a masterful job of capturing the essence of this trilogy. Their translations have retained the self-fuelling flow of the characters' constantly fluctuating language. It was a privilege to engage with them on these plays. Our exchanges were an opportunity to not only revisit the works themselves but also to reflect on a defining period of the theatre. The translators belong to two generations: the late Gen-X which was in its twenties and thirties in the early nineties and the current twenty-something crowd. This, of course, prompted fascinating discussions on how current some of the lines and situations remain and how dated others have become. When we workshopped the translation of *Apocalypse* at Playwrights' Workshop Montreal in the Spring of 2009, I realized to what extent the play, while still pertinent, was very much anchored in a nineties sensibility and stagecraft (particularly because of its heavy video usage). And yet life hasn't fundamentally changed since the nineties, even if individual circumstances have. The economy is cyclical. As was the case during the writing of these three plays, we are again in a recession, but this one is actually hitting everyone hard, whereas the early nineties were especially cruel to youth. With the recent wave of corporate bankruptcies there has been a "democratization" of the un- and under-employed; anyone can now lose their job and their pension. Even the proverbial McJobs are being taken up by seniors. The younger actors and translator felt that the characters' disillusionment at the lack of enticing career options—let alone stability—for university graduates was dated, as their generation has come to expect nothing beyond a life of freelancing and economic instability. If I were to write the drama of twenty-somethings today, I would certainly not use the antiquated answering machine but would play with the multiplicity of communications tools—cell-phones, Facebook, Twitter—subverting them, somehow, in a way that only Ludwig could. I'm happy to leave that problem to today's twenty-somethings.

I don't feel that I "brought Ludwig and Mae to life" but rather that I channelled them from an ambient setting of the errant overeducated youth of the early nineties—I felt like a scribe during much of the time of writing them. Their lines filled numerous notepads over the course of the early nineties, because I could not ignore their voices. I now remember them fondly, but from a safe distance, of course, as they are both engaging and dangerous. Ludwig and Mae consider life in absolute terms: they are intransigent; they are the ultimate Romantic twenty-somethings. Ludwig sought to reinvent himself through fantasy almost daily; he failed as he came to realize that the "transformations" were merely superficial illusions. Mae successfully metamorphosed from victim to empowered author of her own tale by obstinately ploughing ahead towards her younger, more elemental self, resisting the quick fixes of the know-it-all, "been there done that" age. She was able to finally grow beyond that age in a way that Ludwig never could.

—Pointe-Claire, Québec, May 2009